中国思想文化术语多语种对外翻译
标准化建设项目成果
CHINESE THINKING AND CULTURE
MULTILINGUAL TERMINOLOGY DATABASE

中华源 · 河南故事

CHINESE CIVILIZATION
Stories from Henan

# 古都
# ANCIENT CHINESE CAPITALS

主编　孔留安

EDITOR-IN-CHIEF: KONG LIUAN



河南大学出版社
HENAN UNIVERSITY PRESS
· 郑州 ·

图书在版编目（CIP）数据

中华源·河南故事．古都／孔留安主编．— 郑州：
河南大学出版社，2019.3（2021.12重印）
ISBN 978-7-5649-2585-7

Ⅰ．①中… Ⅱ．①孔… Ⅲ．①地方文化－河南－通俗读物②古城－河南－通俗读物 Ⅳ．①G127.61-49 ②K928.5-49

中国版本图书馆CIP数据核字（2019）第047031号

责任编辑 时 娇
责任校对 毛晓旭
封面设计 翟淼淼
出版发行 河南大学出版社
地址：郑州市郑东新区商务外环中华大厦2401号 邮编：450046
电话：0371-86059701（营销部）0371-86059753（大众读物公司）
网址：hupress.henu.edu.cn
排 版 河南博雅彩印有限公司
印 刷 河南博雅彩印有限公司
版 次 2020年1月第1版 印 次 2021年12月第2次印刷
开 本 710 mm×1010 mm 1/16 印 张 11
字 数 156千 定 价 64.50元

## 中华源·河南故事·古都

主　　编　孔留安

副 主 编　薛瑞泽　张　喆

中文撰稿　刘继刚

英文译者　张　优　胡晓军　陈　昊　袁　瑛

英文审校　〔美〕Robert Irelans

## The Editorial Committee
## *Chinese Civilization*
## *Stories from Henan*



## *Chinese Civilization*
## *Stories from Henan*
## *Ancient Chinese Capital*


| | |
|---|---|
| Editor-in-Chief | Kong Liuan |
| Associate Editors-in-Chief | Xue Ruize   Zhang Zhe |
| Writers | Liu Jigang |
| Translators | Zhang You   Hu Xiaojun   Chen Hao |
| | Yuan Ying |
| Translation Proofreader | Robert Irelans(U.S.) |

# 总 序

中国是世界四大文明古国之一，也是世界上唯一的古代文明传统未曾中断的国家。河南省地处中国中东部，是中华文明和中华民族的重要发祥地，在中国五千年的文明史上，河南作为国家政治、经济、文化的中心就长达三千多年。从某种意义上讲，一部河南史就是半部中国史。这里是中华人文始祖黄帝的故乡，是古丝绸之路的东方起点，是少林功夫和陈氏太极的发源地，这里创建了中国历史上最早的都城，镌刻了中国最古老的文字，诞生了中国最初的商业文明。

伴随着新时代的荣光，河南经济社会发展迅速，人民生活水平显著提升，这是自力更生、艰苦奋斗的历史结果，也是对外开放带来的益处。河南经济社会的发展、人民生活方式的改变都植根于深层次的文化积淀。为了让世界更多地了解河南，让河南更好地走向世界，2018年以来，河南省外事办认真研析了这片古老土地上的历史文化资源和时代风貌，组织各领域权威专家学者，编译了“中华源·河南故事”中外文系列丛书，选取少林功夫、太极拳、中医、汉字、文物、焦裕禄、红旗渠、丝绸之路、古都、农业、手工艺等多个主题，力图以故事的方式向世界展现一个立体、全面、真实的河南。

当今世界，人类文明无论在物质还是精神方面都取得了巨大进步，特别是物质的极大丰富是古代世界完全不能想象的。同时，当代人类也面临着许多突出的难题，比如，贫富差距持续扩大，物欲追求奢华无度，个人主义恶性膨胀，社会诚信不断消减，伦理道德每况愈下，人与自然关系日趋紧张，等等。要解决这些难题，不仅需要运用人类今天发现和发展的智慧和力量，而且需要运用人类历史上积累和储存的智慧和力量。河南历史文化底蕴深厚、包容性强，在今天仍极具现实意义。中原文化蕴含的思想智慧有助于修身养性，推动人类社会进步发展，焦裕禄精神、红旗渠精神所体现的为民爱民、艰苦奋斗的价值取向是构建人类命运共同体的力量源泉。我们期待与读者们一起从河南故事中汲取更多的智慧和力量，共同创造更加美好的未来。

# Series Foreword

China is one of the four ancient civilizations in the world, and is also the only country in the world where the ancient civilization has not been interrupted. Located in east-central China, Henan province is an important cradle for the Chinese nation and the Chinese civilization. In the course of the five thousand years of Chinese history, for more than three thousand years it served as the political, economic and cultural center of the country and therefore, as generally accepted, represents half of the history of China. Henan is the native place of Yellow Emperor, the cradle of Chinese culture, the starting point of the ancient Silk Road in the east, and the birthplace of Shaolin Kungfu and Chen-style Taijiquan—typical examples of the world-renowned Chinese martial arts. It was here that the earliest capital city in China was founded, the oldest Chinese characters engraved, and the earliest commerce took shape.

In the new era, Henan has witnessed rapid growth in its economy and remarkable improvement of people's living conditions, owing to the national reform and opening-up policy and unremitting endeavoring of the people. Modern economic achievements and social development as well as the changes of way of life could be traced back to its traditional values and cultural heritages. To enable people from other countries to understand Henan, and let the province integrate more efficiently into the world development, the Foreign Affairs Office of the People's Government of Henan province, has organized teams of authoritative experts and scholars in relevant fields to compile this *Chinese Civilization: Stories from Henan* in Chinese and other foreign languages since 2018, by crystallizing the excellence of traditions and outstanding features of modern development. The book series include *Shaolin Kungfu, Taijiquan, Traditional Chinese Medicine, Chinese Characters, Cultural Heritage, A Model Official — Jiao Yulu, Man-made River — Hongqiqu Canal, the Silk*

*Road, Ancient Chinese Capitals, Handicraft* and *Feeding the People — Agriculture*, etc, attempting to present a panoramic picture of the province.

In today's world, human civilization has made great progress in both material accumulation and cultural and ethical advancement, and the great abundance of materials today, especially, is beyond the imagination of the ancient people. At the same time, however, modern people are also confronted with a lot of problems, such as the widening gap between the rich and the poor, the indulgence in pursuit of luxury and extravagance, the undesirable extension of individualism, the decline of social integrity, and the increasing tension between man and nature. To solve these problems, we need to draw on the wisdom and powers developed today as well as those accumulated in the past. Henan is endowed with a rich historical and cultural heritage characterized by its inclusiveness, and such a heritage remains significant today. The intelligence and wisdom in Henan culture are conducive to self-cultivation and to the promotion of social development. The spirit of serving the people and relentless struggle, as embodied in *Jiao Yulu* and *Hongqiqu Canal*, provides source of strength for building a community with a shared future for mankind. It is our hope that, wisdom and strength from Henan stories, could lead us to a shared brilliant future.

# 前 言

河南是中华文明的主要发源地。中国的古都中，河南占了几乎半数。中国古代83个王朝，在洛阳、开封、安阳、郑州定都的就有33个。河南四大古都各具特色：洛阳定都时间最长，历经王朝最多，遭受战火最重，文物古迹地下遗存最丰富；开封遭受黄河之灾最为惨烈，都城遗址最具特色；安阳殷墟甲骨文最为繁盛，青铜器物最为厚重；郑州作为黄帝之都最为古老，作为中原经济区核心城市又最为年轻。

都城是王朝的政治中心，往往也是一个国家的经济和文化中心。都城在社会发展进程中始终居于主导和引领地位，从这个意义上来说，河南长期引领着中国古代社会的发展。北宋政治家、史学家司马光（1019-1086）曾感慨道："若问古今兴废事，请君只看洛阳城。"当代许多学者都认同"一部河南史，半部中国史"的说法。古代河南曲折发展的轨迹是中华民族命运跌宕起伏的缩影，这与河南长期作为国家都城的所在地密不可分。

# Preface

Henan is an important birthplace of Chinese civilization. Almost half of China's ancient capitals were located in Henan. Of China's 83 dynasties, 33 chose four cities of Henan to set their capitals. Those four cities of Henan were, Luoyang, Kaifeng, Anyang and Zhengzhou. Luoyang was the most enduring of the capital cities, outlasting all other capitals, in terms of duration and the number of dynasties it served. The city was heavily damaged during the civil wars and entered a long period of decline. The ancient remains and cultural relics are still visible today and rank as the top historic and cultural sites of Henan. In Kaifeng, a city that experienced devastating floods along the Yellow River, one finds the most characteristic ruins of the ancient dynasties. Another ancient capital, Anyang, houses a modern museum known for its most impressive collection of oracle bones, consisting of carved turtle shells and ox scapulae, that mark the first evidence of Chinese writing. There are also fine objects from the Bronze Age. Zhengzhou holds its place as the oldest capital built by the Yellow Emperor, and the youngest core city in the Central Plains Economic Zone.

A capital serves as the political center of each dynasty, but also as the economic engine and cultural heartbeat of a country. From the perspective of the capital's dominant and influential position leading social development, Henan played a vital role in the evolution of the power and culture of ancient Chinese society. Sima Guang (1019-1086), a politician and historian of the Northern Song Dynasty, once said, "If you want to know the historical rises and falls in China, just look at the city of Luoyang." Many scholars today agree that Henan bears witness to half of Chinese history. It can be said that from the tortuous development of Henan we may witness the fluctuating fortunes of Chinese nation. From that long history, the long-term roles of Henan's capital cities are inseparably bound.

# 目 录　　Contents

# 第一章

# 十三朝古都——洛阳

# Chapter I

# Luoyang: The Ancient Capital of Thirteen Dynasties

洛阳是河南的一个省辖市，位于河南省的西部，东邻郑州，西接三门峡，北跨黄河与焦作接壤，南与平顶山、南阳相连。洛阳有着5 000多年的文明史、4 000多年的建城史和1 500多年的建都史，从夏朝到后晋，先后有13个王朝在洛阳建都，因此洛阳又有“十三朝古都”之称。

洛阳，古称斟鄩、西亳、洛邑、神都等，是华夏文明和中华民族的发源地之一，是东汉、曹魏、西晋、北魏及隋唐时期丝绸之路的东方起点，是隋唐大运河的中心枢纽。牡丹因洛阳而闻名于世，有“洛阳牡丹甲天下”之称，洛阳更被誉为“千年帝都，牡丹花城”。截至2015年，洛阳拥有三项世界文化遗产，沿洛河两岸存有夏都二里头遗址、偃师商城遗址、西周成周城遗址、东周王城遗址、汉魏洛阳城遗址、隋唐洛阳城遗址等六大都城遗址。

## 第一节　夏都斟鄩，巩固统一

夏朝是中国历史上第一个奴隶制王朝，禹是夏王朝的开创者，虽然当时大禹把都城建在了阳城（今河南登封），但是他的后人却没有一直在这里居住下去。禹年老之时，他的儿子启继承了王位，从此王位世袭制取代了民主禅让制，“公天下”变成了“家天下”。启死后，5个儿子为了争夺王位展开了激烈的斗争，最终王位为其中的一个儿子太康所得，太康把自己的国都定在了斟鄩（今洛阳偃师二里头）。然而不幸的是，太康即位之后，不但没有改善朝政，反而变本加厉，终日打猎游玩。有人向他进谏，劝他以百姓为重，勤于政事，但太康对此置之不理。加上之前夺权斗争造成的内乱，朝中大臣对他很是失望。这样，太康逐渐失去了民心，给了一些觊觎权位已久的诸侯可乘之机。

位于夏王朝东部的东夷族有穷氏部落，在首领后羿的带领下，趁太康外出田猎之时，攻打夏王朝，射杀了太康，取得了夏王朝的统治权。但后羿并没有吸取太康失国的教训，而是像太康一样沉溺于游猎，不理

Luoyang, a provincial city in the western part of Henan Province, is adjacent to Zhengzhou in the east, Sanmenxia in the west, the Yellow River and Jiaozuo in the north, Pingdingshan and Nanyang in the south. Through more than 5,000 years of civilization, Luoyang is a city dating back more than 4,000 years. For 1,500 years of that history it served as a capital city. From the Xia Dynasty to the Later Jin Dynasty, 13 dynasties successively built capitals in Luoyang. Thus, it has earned the title of "Ancient Capital of 13 Dynasties".

Luoyang has been called by many names from ancient times, Zhenxun, Xibo, Luoyi and Shendu. The Silk Road started here during the Eastern Han, Cao Wei, Western Jin, Northern Wei, Sui and Tang dynasties. It was also the central hub of the Grand Canal during the Sui and Tang dynasties. Luoyang is known for the peony. Luoyang peonies still rank as the world's best, so the city is honored not only as "the Thousand-Year Capital" but as "the City of Peonies". As of 2015, Luoyang had been recognized for three world cultural heritages. Along the banks of the Luohe River were excavated the ruins of six ancient capitals including the Erlitou Ruins of the Xia Dynasty, the Yanshi Shang City Ruins, the Chengzhou Ruins of the Western Zhou Dynasty, the Royal City Ruins of the Eastern Zhou Dynasty, the Luoyang Ruins of the Han and Wei dynasties, and the Luoyang Ruins of the Sui and Tang dynasties.

## I. The Earliest Unification: Zhenxun of the Xia Dynasty (2070 BC-1600 BC)

The Xia Dynasty, the first slavery dynasty in Chinese history, was founded by Yu. He built his capital in Yangcheng (modern Dengfeng, Henan), but his descendants did not live there. As Yu grew old, his son Qi inherited the throne. The democratic system, has been replaced, long since, with authority now granted under the hereditary system. After Qi's death, his five sons fought fiercely for the throne. The victor was Taikang who set his capital in Zhenxun (modern Erlitou of Yanshi, Luoyang). Unfortuately, Taikang did little to improve the court affairs and governance. He chose instead to indulge in hunting and traveling. Taikang ignored the entreaties submitted by his officials, urging him to become more visible in public and political affairs. The political climate of civil strife that led to violence before Taikang took power persisted. The court officials withdrew, disappointed. Taikang's

政事。后来，后羿的亲信中有一个叫寒浞的人，伺机杀死了后羿，自己当上了国君。大禹的王位只传了两代就落到了外人的手中。

太康死后，他的后代四散逃亡，他的孙子相被寒浞派人追杀。相死时，其妻后缗身怀有孕，逃回到娘家有仍氏（今山东济宁金乡县境内），生下了儿子少康。少康从小聪明过人，长大后在有仍氏做了牧正，统率一支拥有500人的军队，一面畜牧耕织，一面练兵习武，准备复兴夏王朝的政权。后来少康在其姻亲部族有虞氏（今河南商丘虞城县）和旧臣的帮助下，实力不断壮大。他关心百姓疾苦，与部下一起打猎、习武，深受部下的爱戴。待时机成熟，少康便开始着手部署攻灭寒浞的战争。夏军沿黄河一路浩浩荡荡，挺进河洛地区，直指夏都斟鄩，攻入了寒浞的巢穴。少康乘胜追击，横扫寒浞的残余势力，消灭了有穷氏，重新恢复了夏王朝的统治。

从太康失国到少康夺回政权，夏王朝的统治一度中断了40余年。然而这段时间，大大小小的部落之间经历了多次的兼并战争，为夏王朝日后国土的扩大和部族的融合奠定了基础。夏朝强盛之时，最东边的国土

二里头遗址卫星影像图

The image of Erlitou Site from Satellite

malingering ways lost the trust of the people, and the festering malaise of his rule, opened renewed opportunities for those who coveted his position.

Houyi, leader of the Youqiongshi tribe in the east, and leader of the Dongyi ethnic group, stalked and killed Taikang during a hunting expedition. Houyi became sovereign of the Xia Dynasty. Houyi failed to heed the lessons from Taikang's fall. He indulged in the same obsession that led to the demise of Taikang, hunting. Houyi was fated to meet a similar end: killed by one of his own confidantes, Hanzhuo. The assassin became the new monarch. Yu's throne fell into the hands of outsiders after just two generations.

In the aftermath of Taikang's murder, his descendants and courtiers had fled for their lives. Taikang's grandson Xiang was hunted and slain by Hanzhuo. Xiang's pregnant wife fled, returning to her family in Yourengshi (modern Jinxiang County of Jining in Shandong Province). Back, in the protection of her family, her son Shaokang was born. Shaokang proved his cleverness, even as a boy. He became the officer in charge of a poultry and livestock farm with 500 soldiers under his command. He set out to revitalize the Xia Dynasty, and enforced his will with the assistance of loyal tribesmen and the former officers. Shaokang set out to improve the lives of the common folk. He improved his skill as a huntsman and practiced martial arts with subordinates. For his accomplishments he became deeply honored among the people. Shaokang accepted the honors and prepared for war against Hanzhuo, the assassin who became emperor. Shaokang led his army along the Yellow River near to Heluo. The attack on Zhenxun, Hanzhuo's base and capital of the Xia Dynasty was successful. Shaokang's crushed Hanzhuo's forces and the Youqiongshi group. The Xia Dynasty had been restored.

From Taikang's defeat to its restoration, renamed as Shaokang's of the Xia Dynasty more than 40 years had elapsed. Over the 40 years, there were tribal wars. But rather than spreading chaos, they laid the foundation for the expansion of the Xia Dynasty and for the integration of the tribes. The Xia Dynasty expanded all the way to the sea on its easternmost extension. Its power grew.

Archaeologists have identified the ruins of Zhenxun. In 1959, the Institute of Archaeology of the Chinese Academy of Social Sciences discovered a large metropolitan expanse in Erlitou, Luoyang. The site extended about 2 kilometers from east to west and 1.5 kilometers from north to south. The ruins revealed that

已经到达了大海，势力不断增强。

考古学家们也确定了夏都斟鄩的存在。1959年，中国社会科学院考古研究所在洛阳的二里头发现了一座大型都城遗址，东西约2 000米，南北1 500米，存在时间大约在公元前21世纪到公元前16世纪之间，考古学界认定这里即夏都斟鄩。夏都宫殿区的面积约为12万平方米，外面修建有纵横交错的道路，大路一般宽10余米，最宽处达20米，这是迄今所知中国最早的城市道路网。宫殿区的外围是贵族聚居区和官营手工业区，祭祀活动区则位于宫殿区以北和西北一带。考古学家认为，二里头遗址是迄今可以确认的最早的具有明确规划的都邑。二里头遗址的布局开辟了中国古代都城规划制度的先河。

## 第二节 商都西亳，夏商分界

商朝是继夏之后中国历史上第二个统一的奴隶制王朝，商的开国君主汤推翻夏朝之后，把西亳（今洛阳偃师尸乡沟一带）作为商朝的立国之都。商汤是商部族的首领，他的部族原本受夏王朝的管辖，后来在伊尹等人的辅佐之下逐渐强大起来，通过多次的战争终于成为当时的强国，打败了夏王朝，建立了自己的王朝，并在夏都斟鄩的附近重新修建了一座都城，称为西亳。

商汤在位仅13年便离开了人世，之后依次由太丁、外丙、中壬、太甲继位，伊尹一直作为宰相辅政。商王太甲在执政的第三年，开始变得腐败昏庸，经常越过法律制度任意欺压百姓，横征暴敛，百姓怨声载道。宰相伊尹先是劝谏太甲，希望他能检点自己的行为，但是太甲不听劝告，依然我行我素。于是伊尹以国家利益为重，把太甲放逐到商汤墓所在的桐宫（今偃师西南）。太甲被放逐期间，由伊尹暂时管理国家大事。经过三年的时间，太甲认识到自己的错误，于是伊尹带领文武大臣把他迎回西亳，把政权重新交还给他。太甲再次登上王位之后，吸取

the settlement had existed between the 21st century BC and the 16th century BC. The archaeologists believed they had found the ruins of Zhenxun, capital of the Xia Dynasty. The royal palace covers about 120,000 square meters. There were roads more than 10 meters wide and even 20 meters at their greatest extent. It was the earliest urban road network ever known in China. On the outskirts of the palace area was the settlement inhabited by aristocrats. There was the state-owned handicrafts industrial area. Human sacrifices were made in the north and northwest of the Palace District. Archaeologists believe that the Erlitou site is the earliest and most well-planned capital city, serving as the template for later capitals that came and went throughout Chinese history.

## II. Xibo: The First Capital of the Shang Dynasty (1600 BC-1046 BC)

The Shang Dynasty was the second unified slavery dynasty in Chinese history after the Xia Dynasty. The founding emperor of the Shang Dynasty built the new capital in Xibo (modern Shixianggou area, Luoyang). King Tang ruled the Shang kingdom under the suzerainty of the Xia Dynasty. Later, with Yi Yin's assistance, Tang overwhelmed the Xia Dynasty with the support of a powerful military. Tang

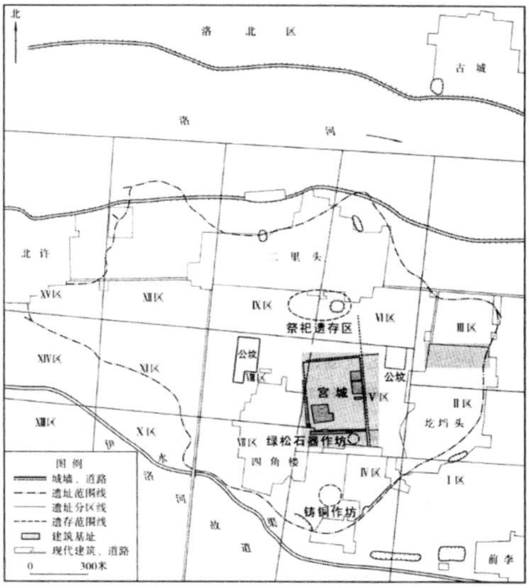


二里头遗址平面图

The Layout of Erlitou Site

了教训，小心谨慎地遵照祖宗的规矩和律法办事，在伊尹等人的协助之下，把国家治理得井井有条。

考古发现也证实偃师商城就是商代早期的都城西亳。1983年，中国社会科学院考古研究所在河南偃师县城西发现了一处商代早期的都城遗址。通过对考古发掘资料和古文献的研究，学者判定这座古城就是商汤所建立的都城西亳。该遗址位于今偃师市市区西部，北依邙山，南临洛河，西距汉魏洛阳故城遗址10千米，西南距夏都斟鄩二里头遗址约6千米。

偃师商城遗址呈刀状，南北长1 700多米，东西最宽处1 200多米，南端仅宽740米，总面积近200万平方米。城址内有大城、小城、宫城三重城墙。大城有多座城门，城外有护城河。小城位于大城内西南部，其西城墙、南城墙与大城西城墙、南城墙重合。宫城位于小城中央偏南，中南部为宫殿建筑遗址，大约占据了宫城的三分之二，宫城的北半部为御苑，是商王休闲游乐的地方。御苑内有人工挖掘并用自然石块砌成的大型池塘，是中国考古发现的最早的引水造景工程。大城的中北部为普通居住区，有制陶作坊、青铜器铸造作坊、小型平房和地穴式建筑。偃

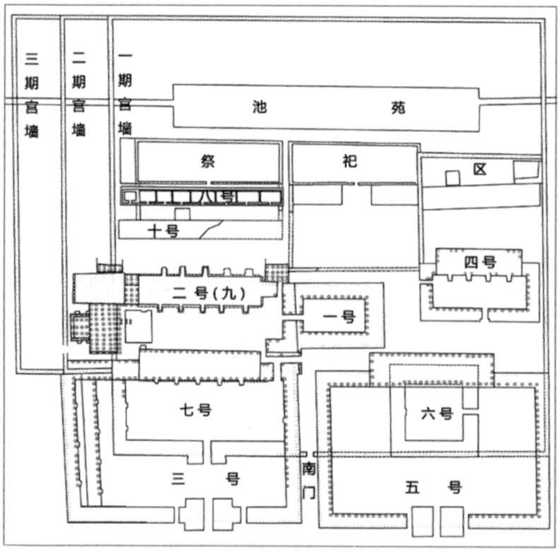


偃师商城宫城平面示意图
The layout of Palace City, Yanshi Shang City

inaugurated a new dynasty in the capital city of Xibo, adjacent to Zhenxun.

Tang's reign was short, lasting only 13 years. He was followed to the throne, in succession by Taiding, Waibing, Zhongren and Taijia. During the period Yi Yin had been prime minister. Commencing with the third year of King Taijia's reign, excessive taxation and political corruption had stirred discord across the country. Without regard to the prime minister's warning, Taijia continued on his own way, until forced into exile by Yi Yin in the national interest. Taijia was exiled to Tonggong (southwest of modern Yanshi, Luoyang), the site of King Tang's tomb. During the exile of the King, Yi Yin took charge of the national affairs temporarily. After three years, Taijia recognized the error of his ways. Yi Yin acknowledged Taijia as a reformed man, and directed civil and military officials to welcome back Taijia to Xibo. Yi Yin restored Taijia to full authority over the regime. After sitting on the throne once again, Taijia had learned his lesson. With Yi Yin's help, he restored the land to order, following the guidance of the ancestors and the law.

Archaeological discoveries have confirmed the Shang city ruins in Yanshi as the remnants of Xibo, the capital of the early Shang Dynasty. In 1983, the Institute of Archaeology of the Chinese Academy of Social Sciences discovered the ruins in the west of Yanshi County, Henan Province. Based on archaeological excavations and historical literature, scholars have confirmed that the city ruins is the ancient capital of Xibo, built by King Tang of the Shang Dynasty. The ruins are located in the west of Yanshi City, north of Mount Mangshan, south of Luohe River, 10 kilometers west of Luoyang Ancient City Ruins of the Han and Wei dynasties, about 6 kilometers southwest of the Zhenxun Ruins.

The Yanshi Shang City ruins cover nearly 2 million square meters. They are 1,700 meters long from north to south, 1,200 meters wide at the widest point, and only 740 meters wide at the south end. The city wall are comprised of three rectangles: a large outer city, a small inner city and an imperial city within the inner city. The large city is encircled by a moat. The small city is in the southwest of the large city, sharing the west and south walls. In the south part of the small town, the remains of palace buildings cover about two-thirds of the palace city. The imperial garden in the north was the recreational area for the King. There was a large, artificial pond made over natural stones. This was the earliest water landscape ever excavated in China. The ordinary residential area in the north-central part of the Large City is comprised

偃师商城宫城三号宫殿南门塾（晚期）
The No.3 palace building at Yanshi Shang City Ruins

师商城内的排水设施完备，排水沟、大渠、支渠一应俱全。

考古学家认为偃师商城是目前发现的早期城址中年代最早、规模甚大、保存最好的一处，是商汤灭夏之后创建的都城。偃师商城小城的创建成为夏商分界的界标，被列为夏商周断代工程的标志性成果之一。

## 第三节 西周成周，双都并行

公元前1046年，武王伐纣取得了决定性的胜利，建立了周王朝。武王选择在伊水、洛水一带建设一座新都。他让自己的弟弟周公旦进行了实地的勘探和测量。周公渡过黄河来到洛邑，考察了涧水以东、瀍水以西的地方，又考察了瀍水以东的地方，认为这里非常适合作为新都城的所在地。于是周公就在上述两个地方分别修建了王城和成周城。王城是王室办公和居住之地，成周城是宗庙所在地，也是管理殷遗民的地方。

西周的都城在镐京（今陕西省西安市长安区），为什么还要在千里之外的洛阳再建一座新都呢？这是因为洛阳具有非常重要的地理位置，

of small bungalows, cave houses, pottery workshops and bronze casting workshops. The City had a well-developed drainage system, including drainage ditches, primary channels and branch channels.

According to Chinese archaeologists, the Shang City ruins in Yanshi are the earliest and best-preserved ancient city ruins so far discovered. This capital city was built in the early Shang Dynasty, after King Tang overthrew the Xia Dynasty. The ruins are recognized as representative of the dividing line between Xia & Shang and are a representative work of the Xia-Shang-Zhou chronology project.

## III. A Tale of Two Capitals: the Western Zhou Dynasty (1046 BC-771 BC)

The last Shang King, Di Xin, fell in 1046 BC. King Wu established the Zhou Dynasty. King Wu chose to build a new capital along the Yihe and Luohe rivers. He sent his younger brother, the Duke of Zhou (Zhou Gong), to make a geological survey. After surveying the banks of the Yellow River, Zhou Gong chose two areas, both of which he considered highly suitable for the new capital. At last, he chose both. He built the new King City (Wangcheng), east of the Jian River and west of the Chan River, to house the royal offices and residence. Chengzhou City, at Luoyi, he raised to east of the Chan River to become the site of the ancestral temple and the residence of adherents to the former Shang Dynasty.

Why did the Western Zhou Dynasty build a new capital in Luoyang? It was thousands of miles from the Zhou capital, Haojing (modern Chang'an County, Shaanxi Province). Luoyang was chosen because of its important geographical position at the center of the Western Zhou Dynasty. Zhou Gong once called Luoyi the center of the world. It was the transportation hub of the country and all transported goods passed through Luoyi. The geographic importance of Luoyi (modern Luoyang) was also justified by the Chinese characters for "Middle Kingdom" (zhong guo) inscribed inside the ritual bronze vessel, He Zun, forged during the early Western Zhou Dynasty. The construction of Luoyi was meant to strengthen the management and control of the country. With territory much larger than the Xia or Shang Dynasty, the Zhou rulers, with their capital far to the west at Haojing, struggled to maintain control over the vast eastern part of the empire.

它处于西周国土的中心地带。周公曾说，洛邑是天下的中心，来自四面八方的货物都要从这里经过。换句话说，洛邑是全国的交通枢纽。有一个名为“何尊”的西周时期的青铜器上也刻有“宅兹中国”的文字，“中国”指的就是洛邑，充分证明了洛阳位于当时全国的中心地带。其实周朝统治者建造洛邑最大的目的是加强对全国的管理和控制。周的国土面积比夏朝和商朝大得多，国都镐京地理位置相对来说比较偏西，无法对广大的东部地区形成有效的控制，于是就决定在地理位置优越的洛邑再建立一座新的都城，采用双都制管理。这是中国政治制度史上的一个伟大的创举。

洛邑成周城是第一座国家层面详细规划建设的都城，从动工到初步落成历时一年之久。周公是这项伟大工程的直接领导者，从城址的选择到都城的建设都全程指挥参与。公元前1039年，洛邑成周城建成。周公将殷人迁移到这里，并派驻军队进行统治与管理。这里驻守着由周王室直接控制的周八师，每师25 00人，共20 000人，用来防御东方。象征着王权的九鼎也放在成周城的明堂之中，用来震慑天下。

由于成周城年代的久远和时代变迁的复杂性，目前还没有明确发现成周城的遗址情况，但考古学家依据文献和考古勘探，基本确定了成周城的位置和基本情况。考古学家认为成周城位于邙山与洛河之间的瀍

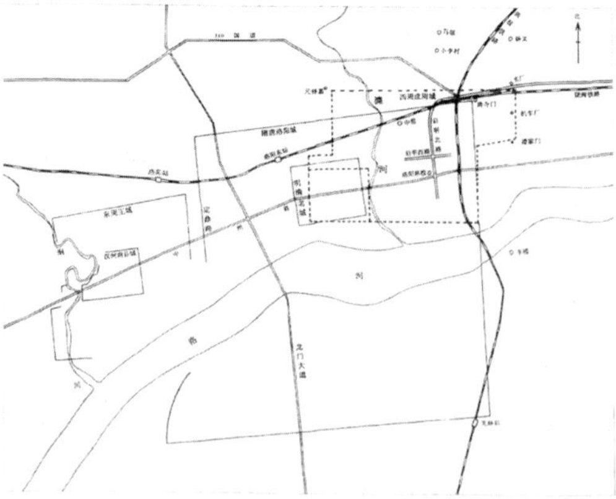

西周成周城位置示意图
Chengzhou City of the Western Zhou Dynasty（1046 BC–771 BC）

Luoyi was chosen for the new capital because of its geographical advantages. The two-capital model adopted by the Zhou Dynasty played a pioneering role in the development of China's political system.

Chengzhou City, a part of Luoyi, is seen as the first capital city at the national level, that was well-planned and constructed. As the chief engineer of the great project, Zhou Gong contributed to the entire process from choosing the location, to the construction, completed within a single year in 1039 BC (the 4th year of the reign of King Cheng of Zhou). Zhou Gong transferred the remnants of Yin to Chengzhou where he garrisoned a large contingent of soldiers to maintain order, under direct rule. In the capital were stationed a troop of 20,000 soldiers under the direct command of the Zhou royal court, to defend the eastern border. The Nine Tripod Cauldrons (Jiu Ding) of the Zhou kings, came to symbolize the authority given the ruler, by the Mandate of Heaven. The vessels, used for ritual sacrifice were enshrined in the Ming Tang (Hall of Light) at Chengzhou.

Although the site of Chengzhou City is yet to be discovered, archaeologists have its general location, based on historical literature and archaeological exploration on both sides of the Chan River, between Mount Mangshan and the Luohe River. The City of Chengzhou was built in two parts: the outer city (Guocheng) and the inner city (Gongcheng). They covered an area equivalent to 12.45 square kilometers of which the inner city occupied 1.56 square kilometers.

## IV. Luoyi: the Chaos of the Eastern Zhou Dynasty(770 BC-256 BC)

The Western Zhou Dynasty came to an end in 770 BC. The Quanrong(a nomadic group active in the northwestern part of China during and after the Zhou Dynasty), overran the capital, Haojing, and burnt the royal buildings to the ground. The newly enthroned King Ping of Zhou, moved his capital to Luoyi (known today as Luoyang, Henan Province). Thus, the previous two-capital system that had distinguished the dynasty became one capital city. Luoyi initially, was built at the beginning of the early Zhou. There were two cities at Luoyi. Chengzhou City had served as the eastern capital. The second city, Wangcheng became King Ping's new capital after the fall of Haojing.

河两岸。成周城的城池分为两层，外面这层是外城，即郭城；里面这层是内城，也就是宫城。成周城宫城的面积大约相当于今天的1.56平方千米，而成周城的总面积大约相当于今天的12.45平方千米。

## 第四节 东周迁洛，乱世纷争

公元前770年，由于犬戎攻破了都城镐京，周平王不得不把国都迁到了洛邑（今河南洛阳市）。平王东迁标志着东周王朝的开始，同时也预示着周代实行的以镐京、洛邑共同为国都的两都制变为以洛邑为唯一都城的国都制度。洛邑本是周初修建，分为两座城，一座是东都洛邑成周城，另一座是王城，此次平王东迁之地就是洛邑的王城。

西周末年，王室衰微，礼崩乐坏，诸侯势力日渐强大。周平王迁到洛邑之后，仍然未能改变这种局面，日益陷入经济衰退和土地减少的双重困境。诸侯不再维护周天子至高无上的地位，也不再听从周天子的号令。各诸侯国为了争夺更多的土地和人口，发动兼并战争，从此开启了春秋战国长达500多年的乱世纷争。

据《春秋》一书记载，242年间，各诸侯国进行的战争达483次，朝聘会盟不少于450次。春秋时期，鲁国朝拜周天子仅有3次，而朝拜齐、晋、楚等国竟达33次之多。周天子“天下共主”的地位已经名存实亡。周朝建立之初，按等级秩序，各诸侯国都城的大小都不得超过周王城的面积。到了东周，尤其是战国时期，许多诸侯国的都城面积都在周王城之上。当时东周王城的面积约为14平方千米，但是齐国都城临淄面积约17平方千米，郑韩故城面积约20平方千米，楚郢都约17平方千米。周王室与诸侯国之间的冲突不断加剧。文献记载，东周初年，周天子为获得郑国的信任，不得不与郑国互相交换质子，沦为和诸侯国一样的地位，标志着天子地位的衰落。公元前707年，周天子率兵与郑国开战，结果周天子被射伤，从此威风扫地。春秋时期，齐桓

The Western Zhou Dynasty was drawing to its end. The Zhou royal family fell into decline. After moving to the east, King Ping of Zhou failed to adapt to the changed circumstances of a vastly reduced land area and the rapid economic decline. As the royal family saw its power decline, its vassals had grown stronger, defeating rival states, and posing a threat to the Zhou. The Zhou kings lost the mastery of the country. The vassal states continued to compete for more land and more people. The vassal states launched a military campaign of mergers and acquisitions. Thus began what became known as the Spring and Autumn Period and the Warring States Period(appox. 770 BC to 221 BC).

According to the book *Spring and Autumn*, from which the era took its name, vassal states launched about 483 wars over 242 years, and established no less than 450 political alliances. During the Spring and Autumn Period, Lu, a vassal state, paid homage to the Zhou royal house only three times, but to the Qi, Jin, Chu and other states it paid homage 33 times. The kings of Zhou had lost almost all political and military power. At the beginning of the Zhou Dynasty, it was decreed, according to hierarchical order, that the capital city of any vassal state must not exceed the size of the Zhou Capital, Wangcheng. During the Eastern Zhou Dynasty, especially during the Warring States Period, that edict no longer held. Wangcheng at the time, occupied about 14 square kilometers. Linzi, capital of Qi, was about 17 square kilometers, the capitals of Zheng and Han about 20 square kilometers, and Chu about 17 square kilometers. Conflicts between the royal house of Zhou and the vassal states intensified. According to the literature, in the early years of the Eastern Zhou Dynasty, the Kings of Zhou were required to exchange hostages with the state of Zheng to maintain trust, marking the decline of the status as low as the vassal states. In 707 BC, the King of Zhou led his troops in battle against Zheng, and subsequently was shot and wounded. During the Spring and Autumn Period, many vassal lords, like Duke Huan of Qi, Duke Wen of Jin, King Zhuang of Chu became increasingly powerful, undermining the influence of the King of Zhou. During the Warring States Period that followed, the territory of Zhou shrank until all that remained was a poor principality that came to its final denouement when it was destroyed by the state of Qin, in 256 BC.

The Wangcheng ruins are located between the north of Mount Mangshan and south of the Luohe River, covering an area whose circumference extends for

公、晋文公、楚庄王等诸侯纷纷称霸，使得周天子成了摆设。战国时期，东周国土面积日渐狭小，偏安一隅，沦为一个贫穷的小公国。公元前256年，东周被秦国所灭。

东周王城遗址北依邙山，南临洛河，平面大体呈正方形，整个王城周长约15千米。王城的宫殿群位于城内的西南角。西北部是手工业作坊区，有制陶的窑场，还有制骨、制玉、制石器的作坊，此外也发现了制造铜器的陶范，意味着制铜作坊的存在；西南部是仓窖区，发现粮窖80余座；东北部是东周王陵所在地，发现东周墓群一处，计墓葬600余座、陪葬坑40座，包括“天子驾六”等规模较大的车马陪葬坑等遗迹。东周王城遗址的发现，为研究周代政治、经济、文化和整个城市的发展史提供了珍贵的实物资料，是中国城市考古的重大收获，具有重要的意义。

## 第五节　汉魏都洛，建中立极

公元25年，刘秀建立了东汉王朝，定都洛阳。中国古代流行五行之说，水火木金土5种元素相生相克。因为历史上的汉王朝是以火德而王的，故忌水，因而将“洛”字的偏旁水去除，改“洛”为“雒”。公元220年，曹丕逼迫汉献帝刘协让帝位，改汉为魏，因其以水德而王，所以改“雒阳”为“洛阳”，定都于此。公元265年，司马炎迫使魏元帝曹奂让位，改国号为晋，史称西晋，定都洛阳。西晋以其强大的军事力量统一了当时处于分裂之中的中国，结束了自东汉末年以来的混乱局面。但由于统治阶级的内部矛盾，加之统治者的腐败无能，在很短的时间内，西晋王朝便土崩瓦解。公元316年，国家又陷于混乱之中，各个民族建立的割据政权纷纷争夺对中原的统治权。公元494年，由鲜卑族建立的北魏政权在孝文帝的率领下，将都城迁至洛阳。东汉至北魏时期，国家从统一走向分裂，在经历短期的统一之后又走向了分裂。虽然

15 kilometers. In the southwest corner of the city lay the palace buildings. In the northwest part, excavators discovered the crafts workshop area, littered with pottery kiln fields and workshops for making bronze, bone and stone products. In the southwestern part, the searchers uncovered the Granary Section, comprised of more than 80 grain pits. In the northeastern part of the city, the researchers discovered 600 tombs and 40 burial pits in the cemetery of the Zhou royal household. A large horse-and-chariot pit was discovered, containing the remains of a six-horse chariot, made for the exclusive use of the King of Zhou. The discovery of the Wangcheng ruins provides valuable material for studying the political, economic, cultural and historical development of the Zhou Dynasty. It is of great significance as representative of Chinese urban archaeology.

## V. The Earliest Forbidden City: Luoyang City of the Han and Wei Dynasties(25 AD-265 AD)

In 25 AD, Liu Xiu established the Eastern Han Dynasty with his capital at Luoyang. According to the Five-Element theory (Wu Xing) of ancient Chinese philosophy, Wood, Earth, Water, Fire and Metal mutually overcome and generate one

东周王城内城外郭示意图
The inner city of Wangcheng, the capital of the Eastern Zhou Dynasty

洛阳一直连续不断地作为帝王的都城，但是战争双方的攻守与争斗，让这座帝王之都在焚毁与重建中历尽了磨难。汉魏时期对洛阳城的建设意义深远。汉魏洛阳城是中国所有都城遗址中，历代定都总时间最长、规模最大且保存较为完整的古城遗址，对后来都城的建筑形制、设计规划影响达千年之久。

汉魏洛阳城是1至6世纪中国七代王朝的都城，位于今洛阳城东15千米，北依邙山，南逾洛水，东据虎牢关，西控函谷关。它是中国古代最大的都城，其城市规模在北魏时达到最大，分为宫城、内城和外郭城三重城圈，面积100平方千米，是西汉长安城的2.6倍、隋唐长安城的1.5倍，比拜占庭帝国首都君士坦丁堡大9倍，比8世纪所建的巴格达城大8.2倍。

北魏的宫城位于城内北部与中部，南北长1 398米，东西宽660米，占全城总面积1/10左右，是最重要的中心建筑区。城的西北隅有曹魏时期修建的金墉城，由3个南北相连的小城组成，平面呈“目”字形，南北长约1 048米，东西宽255米。金墉城北靠邙山，可俯瞰洛阳全城，是进攻和防守的制高点，在城墙的外壁上每隔60—70米就有一座向外突出的墩台，具有军事要塞的功能。

阊阖门是北魏宫城的正门，其北面正对宫城正殿太极殿，南面为御道铜驼街，并直通内城正门宣阳门。阊阖门始建于曹魏明帝时期，西晋、北魏时沿用。作为象征帝王威仪的礼仪性建筑，阊阖门是举行帝王登基、接见四方朝贡者等重大活动的地方，极少用于通行。洛阳市阊阖门遗址是迄今为止考古发掘出的年代最早的都城宫城正门，阊阖门的左右双阙也是迄今为止发掘所见最早的宫城门阙。

太极殿是中国古代著名的宫殿名称。自三国时期魏明帝始建太极殿，直至唐朝，历代皇宫正殿（类似于北京故宫的太和殿）皆命名为太极殿。之后，北宋西京洛阳的大内正殿亦为太极殿，清代北京紫禁城亦有阊阖门、太极殿。太极殿的建造确定了汉魏洛阳城的建筑布局中心，

another. A symbol, the Chinese character "洛(luo)" of Luoyang was set as an augury to maintain the prosperity of the Han Dynasty and nourish it with the Fire, of the Chinese character "雒(luo)". The symbol was altered, however, to remove a radical incorporating the element of water. The Han Dynasty fell, after Cao Pi defeated the numerically superior forces of Emperor Xian, the last ruler of the Eastern Han Dynasty. Emperor Xian was forced to abdicate in favor of Cao Pi in 220 AD. Cao Pi founded the state of Cao Wei and resumed the stroke that had removed the element of water from the character Luo. The Cao Wei state was short-lived. It was defeated in 265 AD by Sima Yan. Cao Huan, the last emperor of the state of Cao Wei, was forced to abdicate. The end of Wei marked the beginning of Jin, known as the Western Jin Dynasty. Once again, Luoyang was chosen as its capital. With its powerful military strength, the Western Jin Dynasty unified China, ending the divisive chaos that broke out at the end of the Eastern Han Dynasty. The Western Jin Dynasty, however, became the instrument of its own destruction. It fell due to internal contradictions among the ruling class and the corruption and incompetence of its rulers. By 316 AD, the country had fallen back into chaos. Separatist regimes established by various ethnic peoples fought for the control over the Central Plains. In 494 AD, the Northern Wei regime established by the Xianbei people moved its capital to Luoyang, under the leadership of Emperor Xiaowen. From the Eastern Han Dynasty (25 AD to 220 AD), to the Northern Wei Dynasty (386 AD-534 AD), the country suffered from repeated unification, followed by disolution and disruption. Luoyang had served continuously as the capital of different dynasties, but it had been ravaged by the wars that saw one regime dispatched to be replaced by another. Of all the ancient capital remains in China, Luoyang City of the Han and Wei dynasties is the largest, most well preserved capital. Luoyang's influence can be seen in the architectural shapes and designs of the China's capital cities through thousands of years.

The ancient Luoyang City of Han and Wei was the seat of power through seven dynasties, from the 1st to the 6th century. It was located 15 kilometers east of the modern Luoyang City, with Mount Mangshan to the north, The Luohe River to the south, Hulao Pass to the east and Hangu Pass to the west. Luoyang was the largest capital city of ancient China. During the Northern Wei Dynasty, the city contained three enclosures: the outer city wall, the inner city wall and the palace city at the

而以太极殿为中心的宫城布局形态，标志着中国古代都城布局进入一个新的历史时期。

汉魏洛阳故城前后延续使用近1 600年，是中国古代最大的都城，都城里坊制以及中国都城建筑的“建中立极”制在此形成，并为后世都城效仿。周汉晋魏风云际会，是中国古代社会形态及文化形态转变的重要时期。罗马帝国与古中国仅有的4次交往，其中有3次在汉魏洛阳故城进行，这座城市见证了中西方文化交往的开始以及陆上丝绸之路第一次延伸到欧洲的过程。2014年6月22日，中国与吉尔吉斯斯坦、哈萨克斯坦三国跨国联合申报的“丝绸之路：长安—天山廊道的路网”项目通过第38届世界遗产委员会审议，汉魏洛阳遗址作为丝绸之路的重要遗址点正式列入《世界遗产名录》。

## 第六节　隋唐洛阳，天人合一

隋朝由隋文帝杨坚在公元581年建立，是中国历史上伟大的王朝之

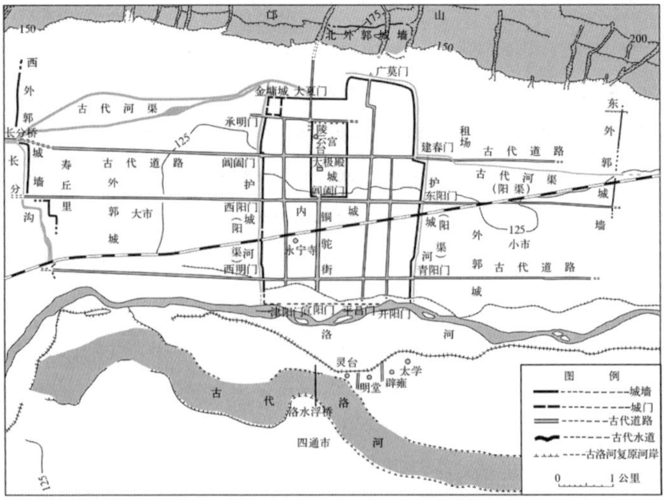


汉魏洛阳城北魏城址勘察平面复原图

The layout of Ancient Luoyang City of the Northern Wei Dynasty

center. The city encompassed an area of 100 square kilometers, making its land area 1.6 times greater than that of Chang'an City, of the Western Han Dynasty, 0.5 times greater than Chang'an City in the Sui and Tang dynasties. Luoyang was 9 times larger than Constantinople of the Byzantine Empire and 8.2 times greater than the city of Baghdad, built in the 8th century.

Located in the north-central part of the city, the Palace Compound extends for 1,398 meters from north to south. Its width extended 660 meters from east to west. The Palace Compound accounted for about 1/10 of the city's total area. The compound is the most important central area. In the northwest corner of the city, the Jinyong Castle was erected during the Cao Wei period. The castle consists of three small cities, linked together, extending about 1,048 meters from north to south and 255 meters from east to west. Jinyong Castle was built on a high hill overlooking the whole city of Luoyang. The protruding towers, every 60 to 70 meters along the wall identify the structure as a military fortress.

Changhe Gate, the front entrance of the Palace City, faces the Taiji Dian (Hall of the Supreme Ultimate) in the north and opens to the Tongtuo Street in the south and continuing to Xuanyang Gate, the main gate of the inner city. It was built during the reign of Emperor Ming in the period of Cao Wei, and remained through the Western Jin Dynasty and the Northern Wei Dynasty. As a ceremonial building symbolizing the emperor's supreme power, Changhe Gate was used only for important events such as the emperors' enthronement and meetings with foreign visitors. The Changhe Gate ruin in Luoyang City is the earliest front gate to an imperial palace ever excavated, and the Que towers ( a free-standing, ceremonial gate tower ) on the left and right are also dated to earliest times.

Taiji Dian (Hall of the Supreme Principle), is a famous palace name of ancient China. Since the Three Kingdoms Period when Emperor Ming of Wei first built the Taiji Dian, the main halls of all later imperial palaces, until the Tang Dynasty, were named Taiji Dian. The name was also used in the imperial palace of the Northern Song Dynasty and the Forbidden City of the Qing Dynasty. The Taiji Dian-centered palace layout, fixed in the Han and Wei dynasties, marked a new architectural landmark in the history of ancient Chinese capital cities.

As the largest capital city in ancient China, the ancient Luoyang of the Han and Wei dynasties existed for nearly 1,600 years, and its "li-fang" system (rectangular

一，统一了分裂多年的中国。隋朝虽然定都在长安，却对洛阳城进行了系统的大规模建设。606年，东都洛阳建成，隋炀帝移宫洛阳，洛阳于是成为全国的政治、经济和文化中心。武则天，唐高宗的皇后，是中国历史上唯一一位女皇帝。公元690年，她改国号为周，定都洛阳。她在位期间，改革政治，休养生息，人民生活在一定程度上得到改善，为唐朝的繁盛奠定了基础。隋唐时期是全世界公认的中国最强盛的时期。

隋唐洛阳城，始建于公元605年，是中古时期世界最大的都市之一。隋唐洛阳城也是隋、唐、五代和北宋时期都城的核心区域所在地，当时中国的政治、经济、文化中心，前后沿用530年之久。

隋唐洛阳城分为外郭城、皇城、宫城、含嘉仓城、圆壁城、曜仪城、东城和上阳宫，外郭城周长27 516米，共有8座城门。东北和南部是坊市居民区，共有103坊。商业贸易集中在城内的南市、西市、北市3个市场，其中北市、南市也是国际商品的主要集散地。为了贸易的便利，全城到处都有水运相通，三个市场的货物都可直接通过船只河流通向大运河。

隋唐洛阳城是按照“天人合一”的理念设计而成的，皇城从东南西三面包围着宫城，与天上的星空、银河形成对应，南北轴线的高大建筑都要用“天”字来命名。武则天对洛阳的营建，改变了洛阳紫微宫中轴线主殿为单层的传统，使洛阳宫城殿宇的立体轮廓和风貌气势显得更加辉煌壮丽。隋唐洛阳城中轴建筑群中的天阙（伊阙）、天街、天门（应天门）、天津（天津桥）、天枢、天宫、天堂“七天建筑”，是中国古代最华丽的中轴建筑群。

隋唐洛阳城见证了中国封建社会最辉煌的一段历史，包含丰富的文化内涵，是研究中国古代都城建制、城市布局、社会生活等方面的宝贵资料，在中国古代都城发展史上具有重要的地位。隋唐洛阳城的平面布局、建筑形制不仅对中国后世影响深远，而且还对东亚各国产生了重大的影响。

北魏洛阳城宫城南区位置图

The southern Palace City of Luoyang of the Northern Wei Dynasty

lanes and alleys), of city-planning and Taiji Dian-centered palace structure, served as the model from the Zhou Dynasty to the Wei and Jin dynasties. Chinese history witnessed great transformation in terms of social and cultural development. According to historical documents, ancient China made direct contact with the Roman Empire on four occasions, three in Luoyang during the Han and Wei dynasties. These encounters marked the beginning of cultural exchanges between China and the West and the earliest extension of the Silk Road into Europe. On June 22, 2014, the World Heritage List added "Silk Roads: the Routes Network of Chang'an-Tianshan Corridor" into cultural heritage project. The project was submitted for consideration by China, Kyrgyzstan, and Kazakhstan. The Luoyang Ruins of the Han and Wei dynasties, at the historic site marking the starting point of the Silk Road was also listed on *The World Heritage List*.

## VI. Sacred Capital: Luoyang City of Sui and Tang Dynasties (581 AD-907 AD)

Founded by Emperor Wen (541 AD-604 AD) in 581 AD, the Sui Dynasty

隋唐洛阳城遗址，位于今洛阳市区及近郊，南望龙门，北依邙山，东逾瀍河，西至涧河，洛水横贯其间，整个遗址面积约47平方千米。隋唐洛阳城的设计者是隋朝著名的建筑学家宇文恺。宇文恺从小就博览群书，熟悉历代典章制度和多种工艺技能，尤其擅长建筑。他亲自参与建造了许多隋代著名的工程，如大兴城、大运河、东都洛阳等。公元605年，隋炀帝迁都洛阳，命令宇文恺营建东都洛阳。他役使200万劳动力，用了10个月时间，建成了这座当时世界上数一数二的大都市。

隋唐洛阳城分为外城、皇城、宫城三重城垣，外城周长28千米，平面呈方形。隋唐洛阳城的外城也叫罗城，对都城起着防护的作用。唐洛阳城是在隋洛阳城的旧址上复建的，为南北长的准矩形里坊式布置的中世纪城堡城市。郭城正南门——定鼎门与天津桥、皇城和宫城轴线贯通，形成洛阳城中轴线。外城城垣的四面共开有8座城门，一般的门宽约7到8米，最宽的定鼎门达28米。定鼎门大街也称天街，是洛阳城的主干道，也是最重要的街道，宽度达116米，最宽处达140多米。城内分布着103个平面呈正方形的坊，边长500到580米不等，每坊的四周都建有转款，墙的正中设立有门，坊的正中设有十字街。城内设有南市、西市、北市三市，是全国著名的贸易市场，其中南市最为繁华。

皇城，又叫太微城，是按照天宫“三垣”中的太微垣来命名的。太微垣是“三垣”的上垣，位于紫微垣的东北方，在北斗之南。太微城是唐王朝的中央机关办公所在地，为都城的外朝。皇城长1 817步（约908.5米），宽1 378步（约689米），周4 930步（约2 465米），城墙高三丈七尺（11米左右），为隋唐两朝面积最大的皇城。

宫城位于皇城的北面，又叫紫微城，武则天时期叫太初宫，是唐朝皇帝举行大典、接见外国使节和皇族宴饮起居之处，相当于明清故宫的内廷。紫微城长1 620步（约810米），宽805步（约425米），周长4 921步（约2 460.5米），城墙高四丈八尺（约15米），其面积和城阙高度均在长安大明宫、太极宫之上。庭院深邃，建筑紧凑，相对排

is one of the great dynasties in Chinese history. Under its rule, the Northern and Southern dynasties were unified. The capital was initially built in Chang'an, but Emperor Yang (569 AD-618 AD) of Sui built an eastern capital in Luoyang, in 606 AD. The new capital was to stand as the political, economic and cultural center of the country. Wu Zetian (624 AD-705 AD), Emperor Gaozong's empress, became the sole, officially recognized empress regnant in Chinese History. In 690 AD, she took the throne of the newly proclaimed Zhou Dynasty (690 AD-705 AD) and moved the capital from Chang'an to Luoyang. During her reign, she reformed political life, stabilized the social order, and improved people's lives, laying the foundation for the prosperity of the Tang Dynasty. The Sui and Tang periods were recognized as the most powerful in Chinese history.

As one of the largest cities of the world during the Middle Ages, the Luoyang City of the Sui and Tang dynasties, built in 605 AD, also served as the capitals of the Five Dynasties (907 AD-960 AD) and the Northern Song Dynasty (960 AD-1127 AD), for 530 years.

The city consists of the Outer City, Imperial City, Palace City, Hanjia Granary Area, Yuanbicheng City, Yaoyi City, the Eastern City and Shangyang Palace. The Outer City has a circumference of 27,516 meters with 8 gates. The northeast and south areas of the city are residential areas, consisting of 103 districts (fang). Commercial transactions were conducted in three markets: the Southern Market, Western Market and Northern Market, of which the Southern and Northern were the main distribution centers for international commodities. The city had a well-developed river system, to facilitate the transportation of goods from the three markets to the Grand Canal.

The Luoyang City of the Sui and Tang dynasties was designed according to the ancient Chinese philosophy acknowledging the Unity of Heaven and Man. The Imperial Palace, as part of the Imperial City, was surrounded from the southeast and west, corresponding to the constellation of stars in the sky. The tall buildings on the north and south axis were all named to incorporate the character "Tian" (Heaven). Especially after Empress Wu Zetian' renovation of Luoyang, the tradition of one-floor main halls along the central axis of Ziwei Palace was abandoned in favour of a multi-floor structure, the three-dimensional outline and style adding to the magnificence of the Palace City. Along the central axis of Luoyang City, Wu Zetian

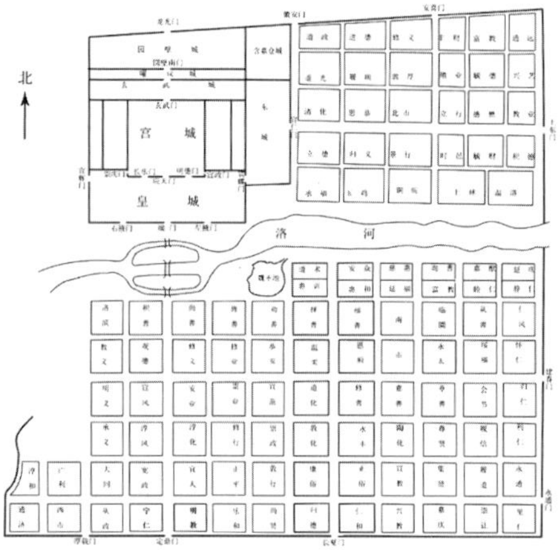


隋唐洛阳城里坊示意图
The li-fang layout of Luoyang City of the Sui and Tang Dynasties

列，秩序井然，幽美而恬静。皇城和宫城是隋唐洛阳都城建筑群中最为壮丽的部分，建筑造型宏伟壮丽，庭院明朗开阔，象征封建政权至高无上的地位。

## 第七节　五代三朝都洛阳，烟消云散瓦砾场

后梁，指五代十国时期的后梁，其建立者是朱温。朱温于907年建立大梁，定都开封，并以洛阳为西都。909年，他迁都洛阳，以开封为东都。朱温称帝后，革除了一些政治积弊，奖励农耕，减轻租赋，基本上统一了黄河中下游地区。但他生性残暴，滥行杀戮，并与据有太原的李克用、李存勖父子连年作战，给百姓带来了深重的灾难。923年，后唐庄宗李存勖攻入开封，杀死后梁末帝，后梁灭亡。

后唐，五代之一，其建立者为后唐庄宗李存勖。后唐从建立到灭亡历时13年（923–936）。923年，李存勖在魏州称帝，同年灭后梁并迁都洛阳。李存勖生性残暴，对百姓横征暴敛，对功臣滥杀无辜，不得人心，其部下李嗣源发动兵变，夺取了汴州（今河南开封）。后来李存勖在洛阳被乱兵杀死，李嗣源进入洛阳称帝，是为明宗。明宗即位后，虽

built seven iconic structures, including the Tianque (Yique), Tianjie (Royal Street), Tianmen (Yingtian Gate), Tianjin (Tianjin Bridge), Tianshu (Honorific Column), Tiantang (Paradise Tower) and Tiangong (the Hall of Brightness).

The Luoyang City of the Sui and Tang dynasties bore witness to the most spectacular period of Chinese feudal society, a period rich with cultural connotations. The layout of the ancient Chinese capital city exerted great influence, on urban planning and social life. It is a valuable subject, worthy of study. The Luoyang city of the Sui and Tang dynasties exerted a profound impact on China's later dynasties, and even beyond, to other East Asian countries.

The Luoyang City ruins of the Sui and Tang dynasties were discovered in the urban and suburban areas of modern Luoyang, with Mount Longmen in the south, Mount Mangshan in the north, the Chanhe River in the east, the Jianhe River in the west, and the Luo River flowing through it. The entire site covers 47 square kilometers. The City was designed by the famous architect Yuwen Kai of the Sui Dynasty. Yuwen Kai read widely as a young man. He became adept at various crafts and studied architectural designs. He was directly involved in many famous construction projects of the Sui Dynasty. Yuwen Kai left his imprint on Daxing City, the Grand Canal, and Luoyang. In 605 AD, Emperor Yang of Sui moved capital to Luoyang, and ordered Yuwen Kai to design Luoyang City as an eastern capital and to oversee the construction. The emperor employed 2 million laborers to complete his world metropolis in ten months.

The square-shaped Luoyang City is made up of the Outer City, the Imperial City and the Palace City. The Outer City is 28 kilometers in circumference, it is also known as Luocheng. The Outer City had a protective function for the capital. During the Tang Dynasty, the City of Luoyang became a rectangular, medieval castle with li-fang urban planning. Along the central axis were built the Dingding Gate (the southern gate of Outer City), Tianjin Bridge, the Imperial City and the Palace City. There are 8 gates on the four sides of the Outer City. The average width of gates is 7-8 meters. The widest, Dingding Gate, is 28 meters. Dingdingmen Street, also known as Heaven Street, is the most important avenue of Luoyang City, 116 meters wide, and at its maximum, about 140 meters. There are 103 square-shaped districts (fang) in the city, 500-580 meters in width. Each fang is surrounded by walls, with a doorway in the middle of each side, leading to the cross street in the heart of the district. There

然采取了一些有效的措施革除弊政，但由于其年老多病，很快就死了。他死之后，儿子李从厚继位，是为闵帝。闵帝无能，934年，部下李从珂自立为帝，是为末帝。末帝即位后不久，石敬瑭勾结契丹攻入洛阳，李从珂自杀，后唐灭亡。

后晋，五代之一，为石敬瑭所建。石敬瑭是后唐明宗李嗣源的女婿，明宗去世前后，他与契丹相勾结，认契丹皇帝耶律德光为父，并将燕云十六州拱手献给契丹，另加岁贡帛30万匹。在契丹的支持下，他于936年在太原称大晋皇帝，史称后晋政权。937年，石敬瑭打败后唐，将都城迁到洛阳。石敬瑭死后，他的养子石重贵继位，石重贵反抗契丹，激起契丹不满，契丹攻打后晋。947年，后晋被契丹政权所灭。

后梁、后唐和后晋时期，洛阳作为都城，战火连绵，政权交替频繁，无暇进行大规模修缮，变得愈加残破，曾经无比壮观辉煌的洛阳城变成残垣断壁的瓦砾之地。宋元明清，虽然王朝一度统一强大，但洛阳再也没有成为国之首都。

## 第八节　佛教入洛阳，白马龙门谱新章

东汉时期佛教传入中国，在洛阳建立了中国第一所佛教寺院——白马寺。白马寺位于河南省洛阳市老城区以东12千米的白马寺镇内，创建于公元68年，是佛教传入中国后兴建的第一座官办寺院，有中国佛教的“祖庭”和“释源”之称，距今已有1900多年的历史。

关于白马寺还有一段神奇的故事。公元64年（东汉永平七年），汉明帝刘庄（刘秀之子）夜宿南宫，梦见一个身高六丈（20米左右）、头顶放光的金人自西方而来，在殿庭飞绕。次日晨，汉明帝将此梦告诉给大臣们，博士傅毅启奏说“西方有神，称为佛，就像您梦到的那样”。汉明帝听罢大喜，派大臣蔡音、秦景等10余人出使西域，拜求佛经、佛法。

are three markets in the city: the Southern Market, Western Market and Northern Market, of which the Southern was the most prosperous.

The Imperial City, also called Taiwei City, is named after the Chinese constellation Taiwei, meaning Supreme Palace. In accordance with Chinese astronomy, the Supreme Palace (Taiwei) enclosure, among the Three Enclosures of the northern sky, lay at the northeast of the Purple Forbidden (Ziwei) enclosure, encircled by all the stars of the Galaxy. Taiwei City was the place where administrative departments and institutions carried out their work. The Imperial City was around 908.5 meters long, 689 meters wide, and 2,465 meters in circumference. With the 11-meter-high city wall, it was the largest imperial city of the Sui and Tang dynasties.

The Palace City, also known as Ziwei City in the north of the Imperial City, was called the Taichu Palace during the reign of Empress Wu Zetian. It was the place where the emperors of the Tang Dynasty held grand ceremonies, met with foreign envoys and celebrated the royal feasts. It served the same function as the inner court of the Forbidden City in the Ming and Qing dynasties. The Ziwei Palace is around 810 meters long, 425 meters wide and 2,460.5 meters in circumference. Surrounded by the 15-meter-high city wall, the size of the area and the height of the city exceed the dimensions of the Daming Palace and Taiji Palace in Chang'an City. The Imperial City and Palace City, characterized by a quiet courtyard and a symmetric layout, are the most magnificent building complexes in the city of Luoyang, dating from the Sui and Tang dynasties. The structures symbolize the supremacy of the feudal regime.

## VII. Luoyang: A City in Turmoil

The Later Liang Dynasty( 907 AD-923 AD) was one of the five dynasties of the Five Dynasties and Ten Kingdoms Period in China. It was founded by Zhu Wen (852 AD-912 AD), in 907 AD with Kaifeng as the principal capital and Luoyang as the western capital. In 909 AD, Zhu Wen moved the capital to Luoyang and designated Kaifeng as the eastern capital. Zhu Wen unified the states along the middle and lower reaches of the Yellow River and reduced taxation, but the thousands of battles against Li Keyong and Li Cunxu inflicted massive devastation, causing great suffering among the local people. In 923 AD, the Later Liang was overthrown, in a

公元65年（永平八年），蔡、秦等人告别帝都，踏上“西天取经”的万里征途。在大月氏国（今阿富汗境至中亚一带），遇到印度高僧摄摩腾、竺法兰，见到了佛经和释迦牟尼白毡像，恳请二位高僧东赴中国弘法布教。公元67年（永平十年），二位印度高僧应邀和东汉使者一道，用两匹白马驮载佛经、佛像同返国都洛阳。汉明帝见到佛经、佛像十分高兴，对二位高僧极为礼重，亲自予以接待，并安排他们在当时负责外交事务的官署鸿胪寺暂住。公元68年（永平十一年），汉明帝敕令在洛阳西雍门外三里御道北兴建僧院，为纪念白马驮经，取名“白马寺”。

在摄摩腾和竺法兰之后，又有多位西方高僧来到白马寺译经，在公元68年以后的150多年时间里，有192部合计395卷佛经在这里译出，白马寺成为当之无愧的中国第一译经道场。

白马寺

White Horse Temple

revolt led by one of its generals, Zhuangzong (personal name Li Cunxu). Zhuangzon, founded the Later Tang Dynasty (923 AD-936 AD).

As with all other dynasties of the Five Dynasties, the Later Tang Dynasty was short-lived, lasting only thirteen years. Li Cunxu himself lived only three years after founding the dynasty. He was killed in the capital Luoyang during the rebellion of Li Siyuan in 926 AD. Internal struggles typified the remaining ten years of the dynasty. The dynasty ended in 936 AD, toppled by Shi Jingtang, son-in-law of Li Siyuan and a fellow Shatuo Turk. The conspirators stormed the capital, Luoyang, with help from Khitan troops. Thus was born the short-lived, Later Jin Dynasty (936 AD-947 AD), in Taiyuan.

Shi's power base was consolidated partly with the help of military aid provided by the Khitan, and in return, Shi Jingtang ceded sixteen border prefectures to the burgeoning Khitan empire. After defeating the Later Tang Dynasty, the Later Jin Dynasty relocated its capital to Luoyang in 937 AD. After the death of Shi Jingtang, his adopted son, Shi Chonggui, became his successor. Shi Chonggui defied the Khitan, provoking an invasion by Khitan. The Later Jin Dynasty was wiped out, in 947 AD.

During the period from the Later Liang Dynasty to the Later Jin Dynasty, Luoyang, as the capital city, suffered heavy damage, amid the battles that saw the rise and fall of dynasties. After that, Luoyang City never regained its lost glory. The country became unified and immensely powerful during the following Song, Yuan, Ming and Qing dynasties, but Luoyang ceased to be the capital of the country.

## VIII. The Buddhist Heritage in Luoyang: the White Horse Temple and the Longmen Grottoes

Buddhism had come to China during the Eastern Han Dynasty. The first Buddhist monastery in China, the White Horse Temple, was built in Luoyang, in 68 AD. It is located 12 kilometers east of the oldest part of modern Luoyang, Henan Province. With its history of more than 1,900 years, the temple is honored as "the Cradle of Buddhism in China".

The legend related to this temple has a direct link to the emergence and spread of Buddhism in China. In 64 AD, on an auspicious day, Emperor Ming (28 AD-

公元250年，印度高僧昙柯迦罗来到白马寺。随后，昙柯迦罗在白马寺译出了第一部汉文佛教戒律《僧祇戒心》。同一时期，安息国僧人昙谛也在白马寺译出了规范僧团组织生活的《昙无德羯磨》。至此，戒律和僧团组织章程都已齐备，一条中土有缘人出家持戒修行的道路铺就，为中土戒律之始。公元260年，一场受戒仪式在白马寺举行，这是一个注定要深深印刻在中国佛教史上的事件。这一天，朱士行依羯磨法登上戒坛，长跪于佛祖面前，成了中国汉族地区第一位正式受过比丘戒的出家人。自此，儒家“身体发肤，受之父母，不敢毁伤”的古老传统被打破。

佛教在中国扎根、传播最初的200年，整个过程都与白马寺息息相关。这里是中国第一次西天求法的产物，是最早来中国传教弘法的僧人的居所；这里诞生了第一部中文佛经和中文戒律，产生了第一个中国汉地僧人。总之，白马寺是与中国佛教的许许多多个“第一”紧紧连在一起的，这让它成为名副其实的中国佛教的“祖庭”和“释源”。

龙门石窟是中国石刻艺术宝库之一，现为世界文化遗产、全国重点文物保护单位，位于河南省洛阳市洛龙区伊河两岸的龙门山与香山上。龙门石窟与莫高窟、云冈石窟、麦积山石窟并称“中国四大石窟”。

龙门石窟开凿于北魏孝文帝年间，之后历经东魏、西魏、北齐、隋、唐、五代、宋等朝代连续大规模营造达400年之久，南北长达1 000米，今存有窟龛2 345个，造像10万余尊，碑刻题记2 800余品。其中“龙门二十品”是书法魏碑精华，褚遂良所书的“伊阙佛龛之碑”则是初唐楷书艺术的典范。

龙门石窟延续时间长，跨越朝代多，以大量的实物形象和文字资料从不同侧面反映了中国古代政治、经济、宗教、文化等许多领域的发展变化，对中国石窟艺术的创新与发展做出了重大贡献，2000年被联合国教科文组织列为世界文化遗产。西山崖壁上有北朝和隋唐时期的大中型洞窟50多个。古阳洞、宾阳中洞、莲花洞、皇甫公窟、魏

75 AD), the second Emperor of the Eastern Han Dynasty, had a dream, in which a saintly person of golden complexion appeared. Behind the vision of the person shone the sun and the moon, coming down from the heaven, near to Emperor Ming' s throne. The throne became circled with light. In the morning, the emperor questioned his advisers about his dream. Royal chronicler Fu Yi interpreted the vision, telling of a divine person, known as the Buddha, who had been born in the westward regions. Emperor Ming forthwith sent Cai Yin and Qin Jing as ambassadors to travel to the westward regions to search for the religion practiced by the Buddha.

In 65 AD, the two set off on an epic journey to the west. After they reached Indoscythae (modern Afghanistan and central Asia), they encountered two Buddhist monks from India. The names of the two monks were Kasyapa Pandita and Bharana Pandita. At the invitation of Cai and Qin, the monks travelled to China, in 67 AD. They carried their Buddhist inscriptionures, relics and their statues of the Buddha on two white horses. Emperor Ming was so pleased to see the Buddhist inscriptionures and statues that he greeted the two monks in person. The monks were accommodated at the Honglu Monastery, the imperial guest house. In 68 AD, the Emperor ordered the construction of a temple outside the Yong Gate of Luoyang. It was named the White Horse Temple, to commemorate the horses that had carried the sutras to China.

In the 150 years after Kasyapa Pandita and Bharana Pandita came to Luoyang, a number of renowned monks from the west came to the White Horse Temple, to translate the sutras. According to historical documents, there were 395 volumes of 192 Buddhist canons. With the translation of those volumes, the White Horse Temple became renowned as the earliest center for Buddhist translation.

In 250 AD, the Venerable Master Dharmakala, from India, came to the White Horse Temple and translated the first Buddhist commandment in Chinese. During the same period, the Venerable Master Dharmasatya, from Parthia (modern Iran), translated an important Buddhist canon about Sangha group regulations. These two translations were seen as the earliest Buddhist precepts in China, guiding those who desired to cultivate the Buddhist way. In 260 AD, the first ordination ceremony was held at White Horse Temple, a landmark in the history of Chinese Buddhism. It was at the ceremony that Buddhist practitioner Zhu Shixing, knelt in front of the Buddha, as he became the first Chinese monk to receive full ordination. Buddhism

龙门石窟
Longmen Grottoes

字洞、普泰洞、火烧洞、慈香窑、路洞等，为北魏时期的代表洞窟；潜溪寺、宾阳南洞、宾阳北洞、敬善寺、摩崖三佛龛、万佛洞、惠简洞、奉先寺、净土堂、龙花寺、极南洞等为唐代代表洞窟。东山全是唐代的窟龛，其中大中型洞窟有20个，如二莲花洞、看经寺洞、大万伍佛洞、高平郡王洞等。

奉先寺，是龙门石窟规模最大、艺术最为精湛的一组摩崖型群雕，因它隶属于当时的皇家寺院奉先寺而俗称“奉先寺”。此窟开凿于唐高宗初年，公元672年（咸亨三年）皇后武则天赞助脂粉钱两万贯，公元675年（上元二年）完工，长宽各30余米，这里共有9尊佛像，中间主佛为卢舍那大佛。据佛经说，卢舍那意即光明遍照。这座佛像通高17.14米，耳朵长达1.9米，佛像面部丰满圆润，头顶为波状形的发纹，双眉弯如新月，有一双秀目，微微凝视着下方。高直的鼻梁，小小的嘴巴，

broke the Confucian precept of filial piety, stating that "a man's body, including hair and skin, which are given by his parents, should be well-protected and kept without harm".

During the 200 years after Buddhism's introduction to China, the White Horse Temple played an important role in popularizing the faith. As the result of China's earliest contact with Buddhism, the temple became the residence of the first group of foreign monks to teach Buddhism in China. The temple also was the place where the first Chinese Buddhist inscriptionures and Chinese commandments were translated, and the first Chinese monk received Buddhist ordination. Because of its pioneering role, the White Horse Temple is honored as the cradle of Chinese Buddhism.

The Longmen Grottoes, located on the cliffs of Mount Longmen and Mount Xiangshan, on both sides of the Yihe River, form some of the most significant and exquisite representations of ancient Chinese stone art. As one of China's State Priority Protected Sites and a heritage monument inscribed on the UNESCO World Heritage List, they are representative of Chinese stone-carving. The Longmen Grottoes are listed among the Four Great Grottoes in China, together with the Mogao Grottoes, the Yungang Grottoes, and the Maiji Mountain Grottoes.

The carving of the Longmen Grottoes commenced during the rule of Emperor Xiaowen of the Northern Wei Dynasty after moving his capital to Luoyang. The work on the sculptures continued on and off for more than 400 years, all through the Eastern Wei Dynasty and into the Song Dynasty. The sculptures are distributed among more than 2,300 caves and niches, carved into the steep limestone cliffs over a distance of 1 kilometre. There are almost 100,000 Buddhist stone statues and 2,800 inscriptions carved on steles. Among these, the Twenty Gems of Longmen Calligraphy and Chu Suiliang's stone tablets are considered rare treasures.

Created over the course of approximately five centuries, beginning in 493 AD, these grottoes, along with the statues and carved inscriptions, provide a window into the political, cultural, religionary and artistic lives of ancient China. In the year 2000, the site was inscribed into the UNESCO World Heritage List. On the West Hill cliffs were carved more than 50 large and medium-sized caves during the Northern Dynasties and the Sui and Tang dynasties. Guyang Cave, Middle Binyang Cave, Lianhua Cave, Huangfu Cave, Weizi Cave, Putai Cave, Huoshao Cave, Cixiang Kiln, Lu Cave, etc., are the representative caves of the Northern Wei Dynasty; Qianxi

露出祥和的笑意。双耳长且略向下垂，下颏圆而略向前突，圆融和谐，安详自在。有人评论说，匠人们在塑造这尊佛像时，把高尚的情操、丰富的感情、开阔的胸怀和典雅的外貌完美地结合在一起，使她具有巨大的艺术魅力。饱经沧桑、老成持重的大弟子迦叶，温顺聪慧的小弟子阿难，表情矜持、雍容华贵的菩萨，英武雄健的天王，咄咄逼人的力士，与主佛卢舍那一起构成了一组极富情态质感的美术群体形象。

奉先寺的9尊佛像的背后有很多长方形的小龛，这是大约在宋、金时代，人们为了保护大像龛，依龛修建了木结构屋檐式建筑，这些建筑影响了佛像的通风，加速了佛像的风化，因而后来被拆除。奉先寺大型艺术群雕以其宏大的规模、精湛的雕刻技艺高踞于中国石刻艺术的巅峰，成为中国石刻艺术的典范之作，也成为唐朝这一伟大时代的象征。

作为北魏时期极具代表性的洞窟，宾阳三洞开凿于北魏时期，是

奉先寺卢舍那大佛

Vairocana Buddha

Temple, South Binyang Cave, North Binyang Cave, Jingshan Temple, the Three Buddhas of the Cliffs, Wanfo Cave, Huijian Cave, Fengxian Temple, Jingtu Hall, Longhua Temple and Jinan Cave are the representative caves of the Tang Dynasty. On the East Hill cliffs were carved 20 large and medium-sized caves during the Tang Dynasty, including the Lotus Cave, Kanjingsi Cave, Dawanwufo Cave, and Gaopingjunwang Cave, etc.

Fengxiansi Cave, the largest of all the caves, is claimed as the ultimate in architectural perfection of the Tang Dynasty. It was named after the royal monastery Fengxian Temple (the Ancestor Worshipping Temple). The cave was carved between 672 AD and 676 AD for Empress Wu Zetian. It is said that Wu Zetian donated twenty-thousand strings of her rouge and powder money to complete the edifice. The monumental shrine has a square plan, measuring about 30 meters on each side. There are nine Buddha statues here. Carved into the center of the rear wall of the cave is a colossal statue of the Vairocana Buddha. According to the Buddhist inscriptionures, Vairocana means "brightness". The Buddha statue is 17.14 meters high, with ears 1.9 meters long. With a plump, dignified and graceful face, crescent eyebrows, downcast eyes, a small smiling mouth and a wise and reserved look, the graceful figure gives the impression of boundless sympathy and concern. It has been remarked that the craftsmen created an idealized image of the sacred by combining noble sentiments and elegant appearance perfectly. The awe-inspiring charm of the Buddha Vairocana remains, as it has done for hundreds of years. The other statues also are vivid, standing out with their different expressions and lifelike appearance, in both appearance and spirit: Ananda is docile and honest; the bodhisattvas are dignified, magnificent and reserved; the heavenly kings are solemn, mighty and strong; the warriors are firm in martial spirit, while the demons are fearless and fraught with rebellion.

There are many small, rectangular plaques on the wall behind the nine statues, carved during the Song and Jin dynasties, to protect the statues beneath wooden eaves. Those structures were dismantled later, to improve ventilation of the Buddha statues. The magnanimous style of the imperial grottoes, as demonstrated in Fengxiansi Cave, represents the supreme level attained in the art of stone-carving in China, and symbolizes the greatness of the Tang Dynasty.

Being of an earlier Northern Wei style, the set of three Binyang Caves (North,

北魏的宣武帝为其父亲孝文帝做功德而建。“宾阳”意为迎接初升的太阳。宾阳三洞开工于公元500年，历时24年，用工达802 366人次，后因为发生宫廷政变以及主持人刘腾病故等原因，计划中的3处洞窟（宾阳中洞、南洞、北洞）仅完成了1处，即宾阳中洞，南洞和北洞都是到初唐才完成了主要造像。

宾阳中洞内为马蹄形平面，穹窿顶，中央雕刻着重瓣大莲花构成的莲花宝盖，莲花周围是8个伎乐天和两个供养天人。它们衣带飘扬，迎风翱翔在莲花宝盖周围，姿态优美动人。释迦牟尼是佛教的创始人，原名叫乔达摩·悉达多，原是古印度净饭王的儿子。他和中国的孔子生活在同一时代，比孔子要年长12岁。他在29岁时出家修行，经过6年，悟道成佛，创立了佛教。由于北魏时期崇尚以瘦为美，所以主佛像释迦牟尼面颊清瘦，脖颈细长，体态修长，衣纹密集，雕刻手法采用的是北魏的平直刀法。由于北魏孝文帝迁都洛阳后实行了一系列的汉化政策，所以洞中主佛的服饰一改云冈石窟佛像那种偏袒右肩式袈裟，而身着宽袍大袖袈裟。释迦牟尼身旁有侍立二弟子、二菩萨。左右壁还各有一铺造像，都是一佛、二菩萨，着褒衣博带袈裟，立于覆莲座上。洞中前壁南北两侧，自上而下有四层精美的浮雕：第一层是以《维摩诘经》故事为题材的浮雕，叫作“维摩变”；第二层是两则佛本生故事；第三层为著名的帝后礼佛图；第四层为“十神王”浮雕像。特别是位于第三层的帝后礼佛图，反映了宫廷的佛事活动，刻画出了佛教徒虔诚、严肃、宁静的心境，造型准确，制作精美，代表了当时生活风俗画的高度发展水平，具有重要的艺术价值和历史价值。非常可惜的是，它们在20世纪三四十年代被盗往国外，分别陈列在美国纽约大都会博物馆和美国堪萨斯州纳尔逊艺术博物馆。

宾阳南洞的洞窟为北魏时期开凿，但洞中几尊主要的佛像都是在初唐完成的。洞中主佛为阿弥陀佛，面相饱满，双肩宽厚，体态丰腴，体现了唐朝以胖为美的风格。宾阳南洞是唐太宗李世民的第四子魏王李泰

Middle and South), was donated by Emperor Xuanwu of the Northern Wei Dynasty in honor of his father, Emperor Xiaowen. Binyang means "greeting the rising sun". Commenced in 500 AD, the Binyang Caves were built over 24 years, by 802,366 labourers. The project was interrupted because of an imperial rebellion and by the death of Liu Teng, the official in charge of the project. Only one cave, the Middle Binyang Cave, was completed, while the remaining two were left incomplete until the early Tang Dynasty.

The ceiling of the Middle Binyang Cave is carved with a canopy in the shape of a lotus flower, surrounded by eight musical apsarases (spirits of the clouds) and two attending apsarases. Their gowns seem to flutter in the air and sway in the wind around the lotus, beautifully and gracefully. Sakyamuni, the founder of Buddhism, formerly known as Gautama Siddhartha, was the son of the ancient Indian King Shuddhodana. Sakyamuni lived in India during the same era as Confucius in China. Sakyamuni was born 12 years before Confucius. He left his home to begin living as an ascetic at the age of 29. After six years, he attained Enlightenment, and became known as the Buddha, or "Awakened One". Since a slim figure was an important standard of the prevailing ideal of beauty during the Northern Wei Dynasty, the Buddha statues always featured a thin face and slender body. The rulers of the Northern Wei regime carried out the policy of the Hanization, teaching the common language and traditions, in order to maintain a stable government amid the central plains. Thereafter, the Buddha's robe in the caves was carved with large sleeves, in contrast to the Yungang Grottoes in which the Buddha's kasaya drops over the left shoulder, leaving the right shoulder bare. Attending Sakyamuni on each side are two disciples and two bodhisattvas. The left and right walls were also carved with figures of the Buddha with two bodhisattvas standing on the lotus base. The north and south sides of the front wall of the cave are embossed with four beautiful reliefs from top to bottom. The top one relates the story of the Vimalaki Sutra; the second relates two stories of Buddha's life; the third is known as "The Emperor and Empress as Donors with Their Court" ; The fourth, the "Ten Deity Kings". In particular, the Emperor and Empress as Donors with Their Court reflects the Buddhist traditions practiced by the court. The imagery portrays the Buddhists' sincere, serious and peaceful state of mind. The relief is of important artistic and historical value in its representation of the high level of relief carving of its time. Regrettably, these were

在北魏废弃的基础上又续凿而成，为其生母长孙皇后做功德而建，属于过渡时期的作品。

万佛洞因洞内南北两侧雕有整齐排列的15 000尊小佛而得名。洞窟呈前后室结构，前室造二力士、二狮子，后室造一佛、二弟子、二菩萨、二天王，是龙门石窟造像组合最完整的洞窟。窟顶有一朵精美的莲花，环绕莲花周围的为一则碑刻题记："大唐永隆元年十一月三十日成，大监姚神表，内道场智运禅师，一万五千尊像一龛。"它说明了该洞窟是在宫中二品女官姚神表和内道场智运禅师的主持下开凿的，完工于唐高宗永隆元年，即680年。洞内主佛为阿弥陀佛，端坐于双层莲花座上，面相丰满圆润，两肩宽厚，简洁流畅的衣纹运用了唐代浑圆刀的雕刻手法。主佛施"无畏印"，表示在天地之间无所畏惧、唯我独尊。主佛端坐在莲花宝座上，在束腰部位雕刻了4位金刚力士，那奋力向上的雄姿与主佛的沉稳形成了鲜明的对比，也更加衬托出主佛的安详。主佛背后还有52朵莲花，每朵莲花上都端坐有一位供养菩萨，她们或坐或侧，或手持莲花，或窃窃私语，神情各异，像是不同少女的群体像。52代表着菩萨从开始修行到最后成佛的阶位，即十信、十住、十行、十回向、十地、等觉、妙觉。

在洞内南北两壁整齐地刻有15 000尊小佛像，每尊只有4厘米高。在南北两壁的壁基上各刻有6位伎乐人，舞伎在悠扬的乐曲声中翩翩起舞，体态轻盈，婀娜多姿。整个洞窟金碧辉煌，向人们展现了西方极乐世界的理想国土，烘托出一种热烈欢快、万众成佛的气氛。

洞口南侧还有一尊菩萨像，她是龙门石窟唐代众多菩萨像的精美范例。菩萨通高85厘米，头部向右倾斜，身体成"S"形的曲线，整个姿态显得非常优美端庄。中国著名戏剧大师梅兰芳早年参观龙门时，被她那优美的形象所吸引并大加赞赏，后经过艺术加工，成功地运用到他的表演中。

莲花洞，因窟顶雕有一朵高浮雕的大莲花而得名，大约开凿于北魏

stolen and smuggled abroad during the 1930s and 1940s. Today they are kept in the Metropolitan Museum of Art in New York and the Nelson Atkins Museum of Art in Kansas City.

The South Binyang Cave was carved during the Northern Wei Dynasty, but several major Buddha statues in the cave were completed during the early Tang Dynasty. The main statue is of an Amitabha, considered representative of the transition from the solemn and majestic Northern Wei sculptures, into the more life-like style of the Tang. It is a cave of merit, built by Prince Li Tai during the Tang Dynasty, in memory of his mother, Empress Zhangsun.

Wanfo Cave is one of the most famous caves in the complex, taking its name, which means ten thousand Buddhas, from the 15,000 small statues of the Buddha in the southern and northern walls of this cave. On the main wall are seven statues, a Buddha, two disciples, two Bodhisattvas and two deity kings. Outside the cave gate are carved two vajras, with two lions beside them. The ceiling of the cave is carved with a beautiful lotus flower surrounded with inscriptions, attesting that the two officials in charge of constructing the cave were women. One was a female official of court, named Yao Shenbiao; the other, a nun named Zhiyun. The cave was completed in the 1st year of Yonglong (680 AD), during the reign of Emperor Gaozong of the Tang Dynasty. The main Buddha Amitabha sitting on the Sumeru throne has a plump face and wide shoulders, wearing a long robe with smooth lines. The characteristic hand gesture known as Fearless Mudra is the Buddhist way of removing fear from the mind and replacing it with inner peace. The four strong Deva Kings decorated on the Sumeru throne are in sharp contrast to the calm and serenity of the Buddha. On the wall behind the Buddha are carved 52 lotuses upon which there are 52 bodhisattvas in different shapes and with individual expressions. The number represents the fifty-two stages in the process of becoming a Buddha. They include ten faiths, ten dwellings, ten actions, ten dedications of merit, ten grounds, as well as universal enlightenment like Buddha and then utmost enlightenment.

On the north and south walls of the cave are 15,000 small carved Buddha statues, each at a height of only four centimeters. Along the bottom of the north and south wall are carved six musicians dancing gracefully to melodious music. The gorgeous cave shows the ideal land of Western Bliss, overtaken by gaiety and joyfulness.

年间。莲花是佛教象征的名物，意为出淤泥而不染。因此，佛教石窟窟顶多以莲花作为装饰，但像莲花洞窟顶这样硕大精美的高浮雕大莲花，在龙门石窟也不多见。莲花周围的飞天体态轻盈，细腰长裙，姿态自如。人民大会堂的莲花顶就是依据此莲花设计而成。

洞内正壁造一佛、二弟子、二菩萨，主像为释迦牟尼立像。这是释迦牟尼的游说像，即释迦牟尼外出讲经说法时的形象。二弟子是浅浮雕，左侧弟子迦叶手持锡杖，可惜其头部早年被盗，现存于法国吉美博物馆。龙门石窟中最小的佛像仅有2厘米高，这些高不盈寸的小千佛位于莲花洞南壁上方，生动细致，栩栩如生。

古阳洞，在龙门山的南段，开凿于公元493年，是龙门石窟造像群中开凿时间最早、佛教内容最丰富、书法艺术最高的一个洞窟。它规模宏伟、气势壮观，洞中北壁刻有楷体“古阳洞”三个字。清末光绪年间，道教在龙门地区兴起，道士见古阳洞无主，不忍荒废，于是将释迦牟尼像改成太上老君道德天尊神像。据传老君曾在此修道炼丹，故而古阳洞又叫老君洞。

古阳洞是由一个天然的石灰岩溶洞开凿而成。窟顶无莲花藻井，地面呈马蹄形。主像释迦牟尼，着双领下垂式袈裟，安详地端坐在方台上。侍立在主佛左侧的是手提宝瓶的观音菩萨，右边的是拿摩尼宝珠的大势至菩萨。

古阳洞大小佛龛多达数百尊，雕造装饰十分华丽，特别是表现在龛的外形、龛楣和龛额的设计上，丰富多彩，变化多端。龛楣上雕造有佛传故事，如释迦牟尼诞生的故事等。

古阳洞是北魏皇室贵族发愿造像最集中的地方。这些达官贵人不惜花费巨资，开凿窟龛，以求广植功德，祈福免灾，而且留下了书法珍品——龙门二十品。古阳洞中就占有十九品，另一品在慈香窑中。龙门二十品是指从北魏时期精选出不同的20块造像题记，它们记载着佛龛的雕凿时间、人物、目的等。这些书法作品的特点是字体端正大方，气势

The Bodhisattva statue on the south side of the entrance, 85 centimeters high, represents the acme of Bodhisattva statues of the Tang Dynasty. Her S-curve shape fully expresses feminine charm and fascination. China's famous master of Beijing Opera, Mei Lanfang paid a visit to Longmen Grottoes in 1957 and saw this statue of Avalokitesvara, taking inspiration from her. He successfully applied her image to the role of goddess in his opera.

Lotus Cave, dated to the Northern Wei period, takes its name from a large lotus flower relief engraved on the ceiling. Lotus is often used as a symbol of Buddhism in China, because the lotus flower grows in muddy water, but is never soiled by the mud. The flower remains fragrant and delightful. Most of the Buddhist grottoes are decorated with lotus flowers, but it is rare to see such large and beautiful lotus flower reliefs, even in the Longmen Grottoes. The lotus flower is surrounded by six flying Apsaras, slim of figure. The design of the lotus on the ceiling of Beijing's Great Hall of the People is inspired by this lotus.

The back wall is occupied by the statue of Sakyamuni, accompanied by two disciples and two bodhisattvas. The Sakyamuni statue in this cave is seen in a standing position, teaching. The two disciples were engraved in shallow-relief, with Kasyapa on the left, holding a stick. Unfortunately, the head of Kasyapa was stolen and is now sitting in the Guimet Museum in France. On the south wall, thousands of small Buddhist niches were cut, vivid and meticulously crafted.

In the southern section of Mount Longmen, the Guyang Cave, the oldest cave dated to 493 AD, represents the highest skill of Buddhist statue carving and calligraphy art of the Northern Wei. The north wall of the cave is engraved with the Chinese calligraphy of "Guyangdong" in the style of regular inscription. During the reign of Guangxu in the late Qing Dynasty, Taoism prevailed in the Longmen area. Since the cave had no patrons or donors to give offerings, the statue of Sakyamuni was changed into Laozi, the Taoist Master, by the Taoist priests. It was said that Laozi used to practice alchemy here, so the Cave was also called Laojun Cave (Laojun as the deified form of Laozi).

The U-shaped Guyang Cave, carved out of natural limestone, has no lotus flower relief on the ceiling. Sitting in the middle of the statues is Sakyamuni wearing a kasaya with loose girdle. Standing on the left side of the main Buddha is the Avalokitesvara with an Amphora vase in hand, and to the right is Mahasthamaprapta

刚健质朴，结体、用笔在汉隶和唐楷之间。清代学者康有为曾大力提倡整个社会书写要用魏碑体。龙门二十品仍有无穷的艺术魅力，每年吸引无数的海外友人漂洋过海，为的是能够目睹这一书法奇珍。

药方洞，因窟门刻有诸多唐代药方而得名。它始凿于北魏晚期，经东魏、北齐，到唐初还仍在雕刻。洞中5尊佛像，身躯硬直少曲线，脖子短粗，身体硕壮，菩萨头冠两旁的带子很长，下垂到胳膊上部。这都是北齐造像的特征。洞门两侧刻有药方150多种，所用药物多是植物、动物和矿物药，药方涉及内科、外科、小儿科、五官科等。所涉及药材在民间都能找到，很大程度上方便了老百姓。药方洞的药方是中国现存最早的石刻药方，对研究中国医药学有重要的作用。

## 第九节　古都洛阳历史名人轶事

洛阳久为国都，在技术、文化、艺术、科技发明等领域名人辈出。他们在自己的时代做出了非凡的业绩，创造了伟大的成就，此谨辑录数人。

### 1. 杜康巧手造美酒

杜康又叫少康，是夏代君主仲康的孙子。很多历史文献都认为杜康是秫酒的创造者。秫酒就是用高粱酿制的酒，后来指用粮食酿造的酒。今洛阳市汝阳县有杜康村，相传为杜康造酒的地方，有杜水（又叫康水）从村边潺潺流过。这里水质清洌，气候适宜，为杜康造酒提供了良好的自然环境。杜康奠定了中国酒品制造业的基础，被后人尊崇为“酿酒鼻祖”和“酒圣”，又被称作“酒祖”。三国时期，曹操在诗中写道：“慨当以慷，忧思难忘。何以解忧？唯有杜康。”高度赞扬了杜康酒的美妙功效。

Bodhisattva with Manichean pearl in hand.

Buddhist niches of various sizes and forms dot the ceiling and walls of this cave. Each niche is distinguished in terms of size, shape and pattern. On the tops of these niches are carved series of Buddhist stories, such as the birth of the Sakyamuni.

Guyang Cave houses the most statues engraved for the royal families of the Northern Wei Dynasty. These dignitaries and nobles spent huge sums to carve the niches, in order to cultivate merits and pray for happiness and well-being. Of the so-called Longmen Twenty Pieces of the model calligraphy, 19 are kept in the cave, with the other at the Cixiang Kiln. They are the selection of 20 pieces of figurative inscriptions from the Northern Wei Dynasty, giving a record of the date, characters and the purpose of each of the Buddist niches. These inscriptions represent the calligraphy style prevailing between the Han and Tang dynasties. Kang Youwei, a famous scholar of the Qing Dynasty, strongly advocated the use of the calligraphy style of the Wei Dynasty. These inscriptions have infinite charm until today, so countless overseas visitors come afar every year to have a close look at these inscriptions.

Yaofang Cave (Pharmacy Cave) takes its name from the medical prescriptions of the Tang Dynasty engraved on both sides of the entrance. The work of cutting of the cave started in the late Northern Wei Dynasty and continued through the Eastern Wei and Northern Qi until the time of the Tang Dynasty. On the main wall of the cave is a group of five Buddhist statues with rigid bodies and showing little definition. They have wide but flat shoulders, extruding chests and bellies. The long bands at the two sides of the crowns fall all the way to the upper arms. These features and styles characterize the statues cut during the Northern Qi Dynasty. On the stone walls of the entrance to the cave are carved more than 150 ancient medical prescriptions. Most of the medicines indicated are plants, animals or minerals. The prescriptions are related to internal medicine, surgery, pediatrics, ENT, etc. The medicines are readily accessible and convenient for the people. The prescriptions are the earliest carved prescriptions kept in China, and they continue playing an important role in the study of Chinese medicine.

## IX. The Famous Historical Figures of Ancient Luoyang

Luoyang, the ancient capital city of 13 dynasties, through its history gave birth

## 2. 老子出关骑青牛

老子（前571—前471）是中国伟大的哲学家和思想家，曾做过周朝管理藏书的官员。他学识渊博，创立了道家学派，他的思辨哲学在世界范围内都产生着深远的影响。他的思想集中体现于《道德经》一书之中，关于这部书的撰写，还有一段神奇的故事。公元前516年，周王室发生内乱，老子受牵连而辞职。他骑一头青牛，出函谷关，意欲西游秦国。离开王都洛邑不远，当他即将到达函谷关时，守城官员关尹见东方紫云聚集，其长三万里，形如飞龙，由东向西滚滚而来，认为此乃圣人将至，于是派人清扫道路四十里，焚香迎候。不久，老子骑青牛来到关下，关尹恳求老子将治世之道著书立说，以造福后世。老子允诺，以王朝兴衰成败、百姓安危祸福为鉴，溯其源，著上下两篇，共约5 000字，合为《道德经》。

## 3. 张衡发明地动仪

张衡（78—139）是东汉时期伟大的天文学家、发明家、文学家。张衡所处的东汉时代地震频繁，据史书记载，自公元92年到公元125年间，共发生了26次大的地震，给国家和人民造成了巨大的损失。为了掌握全国地震动态，他经过长年研究，终于在公元132年发明了世界上第一架地震仪——候风地动仪。地动仪有8个方位，每个方位上均有口含龙珠的龙头，在每条龙头的下方都有一只蟾蜍与其对应。任何一方如有地震发生，该方向龙口所含龙珠即落入蟾蜍口中，由此便可测出发生地震的方向。公元134年12月13日，地动仪的一个龙机突然发动，吐出了铜球，掉进了那个蟾蜍的嘴里。几天后，陇西（今甘肃省天水地区）有人来报，证实那里前几天确实发生了地震，于是人们开始对张衡的高超

to people of exceptional skill, wisdom, artistry, and inventiveness. They are people whose influence exerts a lasting effect on the cultural and political history of China and its present day life. Here is a list of some of the most important historical figures from Luoyang, who made extraordinary achievements in their times.

**1. Winemaker Du Kang**

Du Kang, also called Shaokang, was the grandson of Zhongkang, the monarch of the Xia Dynasty. In many historical documents, Du Kang is credited with the invention of sorghum liquor. Sorghum liquor, produced from sorghum, also appears in later references to wine made from grain. The Du Kang Village in Ruyang County of Luoyang is said to be where Du Kang brewed wine. The clean water of the Du River and the favourable climate of the region provide a good, natural environment for making Dukang wine. Du Kang laid the foundation of China's wine manufacturing industry. Over time, he became honored as the Chinese God of Wine. Cao Cao, the Chancellor of the Han Dynasty, gave high praise to Dukang wine in the poem: "The melancholy my heart begets, comes from cares I cannot forget. Who can unravel these sorrows of mine? I know of only one man, the God of Wine."

**2. Legend of Laozi**

Laozi or Laotze (571 BC-471 BC) was one of China's greatest philosophers whose insights into the "Great Way" are relevant to readers today. Laozi was a keeper of archival records in the court of the Zhou Dynasty. It was he who founded the Taoist School. His speculative philosophy continues to resonate around the world. His masterpiece, *Dao De Jing*, carries a philosophical view closely related to Luoyang. In 516 BC, Laozi resigned his post because of civil strife within the Zhou royal house. He chose to leave his home and travel west to the state of Qin. At Hangu Pass in the west of Luoyang, Guan Yin, the commander of the pass, aware that Laozi was a sage, asked him to write a book to teach the "Tao". Laozi agreed and remained at Hangu Pass for several days. There he wrote his five-thousand-word monograph called the *Dao De Jing*, which thereafter passed from generation to generation and remains in print today.

**3. Zhang Heng's Invention of the Seismoscope**

Zhang Heng (78 AD-139 AD) achieved success as an astronomer, inventor and literary scholar in the Eastern Han Dynasty. During his time, the Eastern Han

技术极为信服。

### 4. 左思创作《三都赋》

左思（约250—305），西晋时期的著名诗人。《晋书·左思传》记载，他曾用10年时间写出《三都赋》，“豪贵之家，竞相传写，洛阳为之纸贵”。左思对自己要求非常高，为写《三都赋》，使得笔笔有着落有根据，他到蜀都、魏都和吴都进行大量的实地调查，收集到丰富的历史、地理、物产、风俗人情的资料。经过10年的努力，这篇凝结着左思甘苦心血的《三都赋》终于写成，得到了当时许多名家的赞赏。由于都城洛阳权贵之家皆争相传抄《三都赋》，遂使纸价上扬，故此有“洛阳纸贵”的说法。

### 5. 香山居士白居易

白居易（772—846），字乐天，唐代新乐府运动的代表人物。他晚年居住洛阳18年，经常与志同道合的好友欢聚在香山寺。会昌六年（846），一代诗人白居易去世，终年75岁，他死后就葬在了寺中，这才有了白园。这座白园位于伊河一侧，与著名的洛阳龙门石窟隔岸相对，园内主要景点有青谷区、乐天堂、诗廊、墓体区、日本书法廊、道时书屋等10余处，这里是全国唯一的以纪念白居易为主题的公园。

### 6. 司马光编纂《资治通鉴》

司马光（1019—1086）是北宋时期著名的政治家、史学家，在洛阳编修了中国历史上第一部编年体通史著作《资治通鉴》。司马光一共花了19年时间，才把这部著作完成。这部书按历史年代编写，从战国时期

Dynasty endured frequent earthquakes, bringing catastrophe to the country and people. According to historical accounts, 26 great earthquakes occurred between 92 AD-125 AD. In order to study the pattern of earthquakes, Zhang Heng invented the world's first seismoscope after many years of research. He named his device the "earthquake weathervane", in 132 AD. His seismoscope for registering earthquakes, apparently had a cylindrical shape, with eight dragons' heads arranged around its upper circumference. Each dragon held a ball in its mouth. Below were eight frogs, each directly under a dragon's head. When there was an earthquake, a ball dropped from the dragon's mouth and was caught in the mouth of a frog. The simple device indicated the direction from which the earthquake had occurred. On December 13, 134 AD, Zhang's device was triggered and a ball dropped into a frog's mouth. The precise location of the earthquake was unknown. Several days later, an imperial messenger arrived to say there had been a major earthquake around 450 kilometres away, in Gansu Province—precisely as Zhang's seismoscope had indicated. Zhang Heng became recognized as a master of technology.

**4. Zuo Si's Poem: The Three Capitals Rhapsody**

Zuo Si (ca.250 AD-305 AD) was a famed poet of the Western Jin Dynasty. *The Biography of Zuo Si*, in *the Book of Jin*, records his most famous poems. *The Three Capitals Rhapsody* (*Sandu Fu*) became so popular that the price of paper in Luoyang rose sharply, as people scrambled to copy his poems as soon as they were released. During the course of writing the poems, Zuo Si undertook field enquiries pertaining to the capitals of the three kingdoms, Shu, Wei and Wu. He collected local history, geography and customs. After ten years of hard work, he finished *The Three Capitals Rhapsody*. The overwhelming popularity of his new works created a shortage of printing paper.

**5. The Hermit of Xiangshan—Bai Juyi**

Bai Juyi (772 AD-846 AD) was a renowned poet of the Tang Dynasty who advocated new-style ballads and folk songs in the style of the Han Dynasty. A resident for 18 years of Luoyang as he grew older, Bai Juyi and his friends often gathered at Xiangshan Temple, earning him the nickname, "Xiangshan Jushi" (the Hermit of Xiangshan). In 846 AD, he died at the age of 75 and was buried in the temple that became known as Bai Garden. The garden is situated on the side of the Yihe River, opposite the Longmen Grottoes. The main attractions in the park are

公元前403年到五代时期公元959年，记载了1 362年的历史。为了编写这本书，司马光花费了大量心血。为了防止自己睡觉过多，耽误编书，他还特意请人用圆木做了一个枕头。睡觉时，只要一翻身，枕头就会滚掉，人也就醒了，这个枕头被称为“警枕”。由于在史学方面做出了贡献，他被认为是中国历史上著名的史学家。

### 7. 程颢、程颐传理学

程颢（1032—1085），又称明道先生。程颐（1033—1107），又称伊川先生。程颢、程颐长期在洛阳讲学，故他们的学说亦被称为洛学。他们的最高哲学范畴是“理”，它作为绝对本体而衍生出宇宙万物。“二程”的理学思想对后世有较大影响，南宋朱熹正是继承和发展了他们的学说，合称为“程朱理学”。

divided among the Green Valley, Letian Hall, the Poem Corridor, the Tomb Area, the Japanese Calligraphy Gallery and the Taoist Book House. Here is the only park to commemorate Bai Juyi.

**6. The First Chronicles of Chinese History: Zizhi Tongjian by Sima Guang**

Sima Guang (1019 AD-1086 AD) was a famed politician and historian of the Northern Song Dynasty. In Luoyang, he compiled the first historiography book of Chinese history *Zizhi Tongjian* (*Comprehensive Mirror to Aid in Government*). It took Sima Guang 19 years to complete his masterpiece, a chronological account examining the 1,362 years of history from the Warring States Period in 403 BC to the Five Dynasties in 959 AD. It was said that Sima Guang was so deeply absorbed in his work that he invented an "alarm pillow" which prevented him from sleeping too long. The wooden pillow was designed to slip from under his head whenever he rolled over. Due to his great contribution to Chinese historical writing, he is considered to be a famed historian in Chinese history.

**7. The Cheng Brothers: Pioneers of Neo-Confucianism**

Cheng Hao (1032 AD-1085 AD), also called Mr. Mingdao, together with his brother Cheng Yi(1033 AD-1107 AD), known as Mr. Yichuan. They often are called the "Two Chengs". Because they were natives of Luoyang and often taught their philosophy in Luoyang, their school of philosophy was called the Luo School. Through the teachings of the Two Chengs, li came to be regarded as the ultimate reality of the universe. Li—defined as the principal, universal law, or truth underlying and governing all existence—was a concept introduced to Neo-Confucianism by the Cheng Brothers. Their philosophy of li later received further development from Zhu Xi. From their mutual efforts grew a major philosophical school of Neo-Confucianism, the Cheng–Zhu school.

第二章

# 八朝古都——开封

Chapter Ⅱ

# Kaifeng: The Ancient Capital of Eight Dynasties

开封市是河南省的一个省辖市，地处豫东平原。历史上，这片神奇的土地先后被称为大梁、夷门、汴州、东京、汴梁、祥符等，它的简称为“汴”。开封的建城史有3 000多年，建都史也有450年，中国第一个奴隶制王朝夏、“战国七雄”的魏国、西汉的诸侯国梁国、五代时期的梁晋汉周、北宋王朝、金朝以及元末的红巾军韩林儿政权等都在此建都。开封有个特点，就是城套城、城摞城，不同历史时期的开封城一个套一个，一个压一个，现在的开封城位置最高，它的底下有许多古城存在着。历史上，开封与黄河的关系剪不断理还乱，有时它得到黄河的恩赐，发展迅猛，有时它又受到黄河的惩罚，一落千丈。开封地势平旷，交通便利，物产丰富，是个不可多得的宜居之地。古人曾用“汴京富丽天下无”来赞美这个美丽富庶的城市。

## 第一节　开拓封疆，原为启封

“开封”一名，实际来源于春秋时期的启封，这里面还有个美好的故事。春秋时期，郑庄公作为郑国的第三代国君，雄心勃勃，意欲兼并诸侯，称霸中原。他选中了现在朱仙镇古城村一带用以囤积粮草和操练士兵，因为他有“启拓封疆”之意，所以就把这个地方叫作“启封”。这片土地东临宋国，北接卫国，南与陈、蔡接壤，地理位置十分重要。从那时起，一直到唐代初年，位于今开封市西南约25千米的开封县朱仙镇古城村就是我们所说的“开封”。那它又为什么叫开封呢？原来当历史的车轮来到西汉时，汉景帝的名字与启封有了交集。汉景帝叫刘启，“启封”中也有个“启”字，这就犯了忌讳了，所以为了避讳，启封就无奈地改成了开封。

由于黄河淹没，启封故城如今只有西墙一段100多米的残垣尚存，它高约7米，宽30米。1975年，湖北云梦睡虎地秦墓中出土的一批秦

Kaifeng, a provincially governed city in Henan Province, is located on the East Henan Plain. Historically, this mysterious land has been known by different names: Daliang, Yimen, Bianzhou, Dongjing, Bianliang and Xiangfu. Today the land, conventionally, is known as "Bian", for short. Kaifeng has a history extending over 3,000 years, and for 450 years of that, it was the location of many of China's ancient Capitals. These high points of Bian's history came during the Xia Dynasty, as the capital of China's first slavery political entity; the Wei Dynasty, one of "The Seven Powers of the Warring States Period"; Liang of the Western Han; the Five Dynasties Period of Liang, Jin, Han and Zhou; the Northern Song Dynasty; the Jin Dynasty and the Hanliner regime of the Red Turbans of the later Yuan Dynasty. Kaifeng is typically characterized by its distinctive mode of construction planning. A new castle would be built on the site where the old fell, through war or natural disaster. Lying beneath the ground of Kaifeng are the ruins of many ancient castles. Historically, the rise and fall of Kaifeng was closely linked to the Yellow River. Sometimes, the city grew rapidly when well-nourished by the river; at other times, the river rushed away as if cursed by Nature. Kaifeng is a favourable location for human settlement, because of the flat surrounding plain, convenient transportation and abundant resources. It has earned the praise "Nothing can compete with the beauty and prosperity of Bianjing".

## I. Qifeng: the Original Name of Kaifeng

The city name of Kaifeng is, in fact, derived from Qifeng of the Spring and Autumn Period. During the Spring and Autumn Period, Duke Zhuang of Zheng, as the third-generation ruler of the state of Zheng, set out to fulfill his ambition to unify the fragmented parts of China into one empire. He selected the Gucheng Village, in Zhuxian Town, as the base for a food stockpile and for training of the army. In the pursuit of "exploring and expanding the territory", the selected area was called "Qifeng". Why was it so named? There is an interesting story about the name. The territory was bounded by the state of Song to the east, the state of Wei to the north, the states of Chen and Cai to the south. Kaifeng was at the center of a strong geographical and strategic location. Up to the early Tang Dynasty, what is now Gucheng village lay 25 kilometres distant from Kaifeng. Why was it renamed Kaifeng? In the Western Han Dynasty, the name of Emperor Jing had the same character "Qi", as the character in the city name of Qifeng—but

启封故城

Qifeng City

简中有秦昭襄王“攻启封”的记载。司马迁在《史记》中也记载有“开封”二字，这样就得到了互相印证。如今这段古老的城墙静静地矗立在中原大地上，似乎在诉说着过去的荣光，呼唤人们关心古都的变迁，重视古都的发展。

## 第二节　夏都老丘，依稀朦胧

老丘，夏代的都城，这是开封作为都城的第一个名字。那么古书中的老丘真的就是今天的开封吗？《大清一统志·开封府》引《太平寰宇记》说，老丘城“在陈留县北四十五里”。另一本书《古史纪年》引《春秋地名考》说：“老丘，古地名，在今河南陈留城北。”经过考古工作者的研究，距开封市东北约 20 千米，陈留镇北 19.2 千米的国都里村就是古代的夏都老丘。

the character Qi was forbidden from use in the naming of the city. Finally, the name Qifeng was changed to Kaifeng.

Owing to the flooding of the Yellow River, all that remains of the ancient castle wall of Qifeng is a section, of almost 100m in length, 7m in height, 30m in width. Bamboo inscriptions of the Qin Dynasty, unearthed from the tomb of Qin, in Yunmeng County, Hubei Province, in 1975, record an attack on Qifeng. Kaifeng was also mentioned in Sima Qian's great historical book, *Shi Ji* (*Records of the Historian*). Nowadays, the remains of the ancient wall, extending across the Central Plains, serve as a reminder of past glories. There are public concerns about changing the site, and fears of changes and even re-development of the ancient city.

## II. Laoqiu: the Capital of the Xia Dynasty

Conventional wisdom holds that Laoqiu was the original name of Kaifeng, dating back to when it was the capital of the Xia Dynasty. This conviction is drawn from ancient literature. It is recorded in *The Total Annals of the Qing Dynasty—Kaifeng City*, cited from *Taiping Geographical Record*, that Laoqiu was located 45 miles to the north of Chenliu County. Another book, *Annals of Ancient Chinese History* quoted *The Names of Places during the Spring and Autumn Period*, in which "Laoqiu, an ancient place, is located to the north of Chenliu county in Henan". Archaeological studies reveal that Guoduli village, which is about 20 kilometers away from Kaifeng and 19.2 kilometers to the north of Chenliu Town, is Laoqiu, the capital of the Xia Dynasty.

In the spring of 1998, archaeologists in Kaifeng conducted archaeological explorations in Guoduli village, and discovered a large ancient cultural site. The site is more than 3 meters above ground, and the cultural layer is up to 11 meters below ground. Some of the pottery fragments are characteristic of the Xia and Shang cultures. Without guidance from written records, archaeologists were able to reproduce a representative image of Laoqiu.

Kaifeng itself is located at the end of the alluvial fan of the Yellow River. The elevation of the terrain is generally high in the west and low in the east. It rises in the north and falls in the south. During the Holocene Period, the climate grew warmer and the precipitation increased. The rivers around Kaifeng flowed east or southeast.

1998年春天，开封市考古工作者对国都里村进行了考古钻探，结果勘探出了一处大型古文化遗址。这处遗址高出地面3米多，文化层堆积深达11米，探出的一些破碎陶片具有明显的夏商文化特征。由于没有文字记载，我们只能依靠考古上的证据去想象。

开封位于黄河冲积扇的末端，地势总体西高东低，北起南伏。全新世时期，气候日益变暖，降水增多，开封周围的自然河流向东或东南流淌，日久天长，就形成了开封附近河、泽、丘、冈密布相间的地貌形态。这里河流纵横，水泽密布，草木繁茂，是中国先民们耕作、渔猎的理想场所。但是，历史上这里水患极多，先民们往往选择高冈之处安居。夏朝的第7个帝叫杼，他本来领着部族在原地居住，原地在今河南济源西北。后来，他从原地迁到老丘这个地方，到第13个帝胤甲时才又迁到西河这个地方。算起来，历经六世，夏代在老丘建都时间近200年。国都里村由来已久，历代立碑相传，现在该村东北角一带还高出地面，可见当时夏代的统治者已懂得在高处安居，避免水患。当时，开封周围水泽密布，东南有逢泽，西有圃田泽，东北有巨野泽，整体地势低湿。

## 第三节 魏都大梁，国富民强

大梁城，魏国的都城。历史进入到战国时期，魏国为了更好地发展，公元前364年（魏惠王六年），魏惠王就把国都从安邑迁到了大梁城。今天的开封市有确切文献记载的历史，就是从这一年开始的。作为大国都城，开封也进入了一个新的重要的发展时期。

大梁城规模宏大。城内有许多巍峨壮丽的宫殿和穷奢极欲的苑囿，比如兰台、京台、晖台、范台和梁囿等。刘向在《战国策》里多次提及这些富丽堂皇的处所，他还着重提到梁囿这个地方。

大梁城文化发达，名人辈出，令人惊叹。魏公子信陵君“窃符救赵”，

Over millennia, the present day geomorphological pattern of rivers, mountains, hills and ridges was formed. In addition to abundant waters and lush vegetation along the riverbanks, the region became an ideal place for the ancestors of present-day Chinese to cultivate, fish and hunt. History records frequent flooding, providing the likely reason for ancient peoples to build their dwellings on high ground. The seventh emperor of the Xia Dynasty was Zhu. It was he who led his tribe to the northwest of Jiyuan, Henan. Later, he relocated to Laoqiu(Kaifeng). The thirteenth emperor moved to the Xihe area. Laoqiu was the center of six dynasties. It served the Xia for nearly 200 years. Guoduli Village has a long history. Its historical record has passed down from generation to generation. People still live in the village, on higher ground built up over the centuries, above the remains of settlements dating back hundreds of years. It can be seen that the rulers of the Xia Dynasty recognized the importance of high ground to avoid devastation from floods. In the Xia Era, there were dense marshes around Kaifeng, including Fengze Marsh in the southeast, Putianze Marsh in the west, and Juyeze Marsh in the northeast. Much of the terrain was low and moist.

## III. Daliang: A Prosperous Capital of Wei

Daliang was the capital of the Wei Dynasty during the Warring States Period. King Hui of Wei moved his capital to Daliang from Anyi in 364 BC for the better growth of the empire. Daliang lies in close proximity to Kaifeng, (often Daliang is referred to as Kaifeng) and there is well-documented history of the times when Daliang was the capital of the Wei. As the capital of a great power, Kaifeng entered an important stage of development.

The Daliang City was immense. It boasted magnificent palaces and gardens: Lantai, Jingtai, Huitai, Fantai and Liangyou, etc. In *Zhanguo Ce* (*Intrigues of the Warring States*), Liu Xiang mentioned these splendid places many times. He also highlighted Liangyou.

Daliang's culture flourished and attracted leading figures. After Lord Xinling had rescued Zhao, whose capital Handan had been under siege by the Qin, figures exalted throughout history arrived. They included Hou Ying, Zhu Hai, Ru Ji and Jin Bi. The renowned musician Shi Kuang performed here. The philosopher Meng Zi persuaded King Hui of Liang to do good and to adopt a policy of benevolence.

义薄云天，侯嬴、朱亥、如姬、晋鄙等人物形象千百年来众口传诵。大音乐家师旷曾在此演奏，大思想家孟子在此劝梁惠王行仁义、施仁政。魏公子信陵君编著有《魏公子兵法》，尉缭子作为大梁人也留下一部杰出的军事著作《尉缭子》。大梁人石申是中国最早的天文学家，他同甘德一起详尽记录了120颗恒星的赤道坐标。他们二人所测定的恒星表，是世界上最古老的恒星表。这些政治、军事、科技、艺术人才使古大梁城在历史的星空中闪闪发光。

战国名都的余晖，毕竟遮不住大梁城的无穷魅力。当历史来到汉代时，这里成为一个诸侯国的统治中心。汉初实行郡国制，从汉高祖刘邦开始，在西汉的政治版图中就一直有梁国的存在。只是由于战争的影响，从彭越开始，历任梁王都未选择大梁作为都城。直到汉文帝时，刘武为梁王定都大梁，不过这时的大梁也改了个新的名字——浚仪。梁孝王刘武虽然在这里待的时间不长，就又把他的梁国都城迁到了睢阳，也就是今天的商丘，但是，相传他在这里修建了一座规模宏大的梁园。园内既有广袤的森林，也有众多的楼台，梁孝王与其宾客在此游乐。梁园也叫梁苑、竹园，许多文人学子对此作过描绘，如李白有《梁园吟》，王昌龄有《梁苑》等诗篇，岑参也曾用“君不见梁孝王修竹园，颓墙隐辚势仍存”来咏叹梁园。

## 第四节　五代时期，开封地位日益升

唐朝末年，朱温于907年在开封称帝，建国号为梁，史称后梁。在其称帝诏书中这样写道：“宜升汴州为开封府，建名东都。其东都改为西都，仍废京兆府为雍州佑国军节度使。”这里改为西都的东都指的是洛阳，废为雍州佑国军的京兆府为长安。可见开封、洛阳、西安这三个城市在当时的地位升降，开封已从唐代的汴州这个地方城市成为后梁的

Lord Xinling wrote the *Wei Gongzi's Art of War*, and Wei Liaozi as a Liangnese, left an outstanding military work of *Wei Liaozi*. The Liangnese, Shi Shen, was the earliest astronomer in China. He and Gan De gave a detailed account of equatorial coordinates of 120 stars. Their sidereal table is the oldest in the world. These political, military, scientific and artistic talents made magnificent contributions to Daliang.

The glory of well-known capitals in the period of the Warring States Period can't surpass the infinite charm of Daliang. During the Han Dynasty, it became a ruling center of lords. The system of counties and prefectures was implemented in the early stages of the Han Dynasty. Under the rule of Liu Bang, Liang had been marked on the political map of the Western Han. It was only because of the constant wars that the successive kings of Liang had not chosen Daliang as their capital since the rulership of Peng Yue. When emperor Wen of Han came to power, his son, Prince Liu Wu chose Daliang as the capital, and changed the name to Junyi. Although Liu Wu remained for a short time at Daliang, he later removed the capital to Suiyang (now Shangqiu). According to legend, he built a large-scale Liang garden, consisting of vast forests and numerous buildings, where Liu Wu, later known as King Xiao of Liang, often invited guests for recreation. Liang Garden is also called Liang Yuan or Bamboo Garden. Many poets described it in their works. References can be found in Li Bai's and Wang Changling's. Cen Sen sighed that no one witnessed the building of the Bamboo Garden, but the ruins were left in evidence.

## IV. The Rising of Kaifeng in the Five Dynasties

At the end of the Tang Dynasty, Zhu Wen proclaimed himself emperor in Kaifeng in 907 AD. The period is known historically as "Later Liang". The imperial edict read, "Bian Zhou was the Kaifeng Prefecture, which was also called Dongdu. Dongdu was renamed as Xidu, while the Jingzhao Prefecture was abolished. "Here Dongdu is what is now Luoyang, and the abolished Jingzhao Prefecture is what is now Chang'an. It can be seen that Kaifeng, Luoyang and Xi'an were not in the same position in order of magnitude. After Tang, Kaifeng changed from Bian to Dongdu, as the capital of the Later Liang Dynasty. It is no doubt that the change reflects the inevitable trend of historical development and the city's growing prosperity.

The famous Beijing-Hangzhou Canal was built during the Sui Dynasty. One

东都了。这种变化不是没有来由的，它是历史发展的必然趋势。

隋代修建了中国历史上闻名的京杭大运河，这条运河有一段叫通济渠，它连接了黄河与淮河，贯通了洛阳与扬州，因隋炀帝杨广多次在这条河上游玩，在当时也被称为“御河”。唐朝时，通济渠被称为汴河。开封恰在汴河之上，地位极其独特。安史之乱后，长安和洛阳几乎沦为废墟，中国北部的许多城市也受到严重的破坏，开封由于其独特的地位却不断发展壮大。

朱温称帝前曾为宣武军节度使，其治所就在开封，当时称为汴州。他不断扩大地盘发展势力，汴州在唐末已逐渐成为当时的政治中心。由于汴州独特的交通枢纽地位，它的经济实力也越来越强。这是因为安史之乱后，唐代的藩镇割据之势已经形成，北方的财政收入基本上被一些割据的藩镇扣留，唐王朝无力要回，只有依赖江南转运的赋税来维持政府各项开支。

开封的城市建设也得到加强。公元 781 年，唐王朝重筑汴州城，修筑其外城。此时，汴州城有 7 座城门，周围长约 10 077.5 米，并且把汴河围入了城内，还修筑了著名的汴州桥，简称为“州桥”，重建了相国寺。许多名人也来这里游览，留下了许多佳话。画家吴道子和雕塑家杨惠之在相国寺留下了壁画和塑像，李白、杜甫和高适在这里游览赋诗，成为文坛佳话。日本的弘法大师曾在相国寺居住，开封见证了中日之间的佛学交流。开封成为后梁的东都后，城市建设方面进一步得到了加强，修建皇宫以供帝王居住，修筑皇家的宗庙社稷坛等，加强其政治中心地位。

后唐灭后梁后，定都洛阳，开封被降为汴州宣武军节度使，又成为一个地区性城市。后晋灭后唐后，经过比较洛阳与开封的利弊后，仍然定都于开封。后晋高祖石敬瑭先改汴州宫室为大宁宫，接着下诏：“汴州宜升为东京，置开封府。”开封在五代这个乱世第二次成为国都，也是首次被称为“东京”。历史经过螺旋式发展，又回到了起点，开封的

section of the canal, called Tongji Canal, connects the Yellow River and Huaihe River and traverses Luoyang and Yangzhou. The Emperor, Yang Guang, travelled many times along the upper course of the river, known as the Yuhe. During the Tang Dynasty, Tongji Canal was known as the Bianhe River. Kaifeng with its unique geographic characteristics was located along the Bianhe River. After the An Shi Rebellion, Chang'an and Luoyang fell nearly to ruin, while many other cities in northern China were severely damaged. Kaifeng survived and continued to evolve because of its geographical position.

Before becoming emperor in 907 AD, Zhu Wen was assigned as governor of the Xuanwu Army in Kaifeng, then known as Bianzhou. He continued to expand the territory and to improve its military strength. Bianzhou gradually became the political center of the era. Owing to its standing as a vital transportation hub, the city's economy grew. After the An Shi Rebellion, many local military governors had gained significant autonomy. Most of the fiscal revenues of North China were withheld by the governors. The Tang Dynasty was unable to re-acquire the lost revenue and had to rely on taxes from the south to maintain expenses.

Kaifeng greatly developed during the Tang Dynasty. In 781 AD, Bianzhou was reconstructed with new outer walls. Bianzhou, with seven gates, extended over 10,077.5 meters in circumference. The Bianhe River was enclosed by the walls. The famous Bianzhou Bridge, referred as the "Zhou Bridge", was constructed and the Xiangguo Temple was rebuilt. Persons of acclaim travelled there and told many tales of their exciting adventures. The painter Wu Daozi and the sculptor Yang Huizhi, left masterpieces in murals and sculptures in Xiangguo Temple. Li Bai, Du Fu and Gao Shi travelled there and wrote rich poetry, still well known in the field of literature. The Japanese master of Kobo Daishi (774 AD-835 AD), once lived at Xiangguo Temple, and Kaifeng was witness to the Buddhist exchange between China and Japan. After Kaifeng, renamed Dongdu, became the capital of the Later Liang Dynasty, urban construction accelerated. The palace was built to serve as the emperor's residence. The royal ancestral temple was built to enhance the city's status as the political center.

After the Later Liang Dynasty declined, the Later Tang Dynasty chose Luoyang as its capital. Kaifeng was downgraded to become the administrative center of the local army in Bianzhou and then became a regional city. After the Later Tang Dynasty was taken over by the Later Jin Dynasty, Kaifeng was reinstated as the

政治中心地位得到了巩固。后汉灭后晋，继续定都开封。后周灭后汉后，仍然定都开封。五代时期一共 50 多年，除后唐外，其他王朝都定都于开封，开封成为都城的时间达 40 年之久。从五代的定都史来看，它已完全取代长安和洛阳，成为新的政治中心。

后周时期，政治较为稳定，开封的城市建设得到加强。一是兴修外城，周围长约 24 116.5 米。二是拓宽街道，拆除临街坊墙，方便交通。这样就解决了建设用地不足、交通不便等问题，使得开封成为一个像模像样的都城。周世宗还整治了开封城对外的水路交通，疏导汴河，使其直通淮河，北入五丈河，使齐鲁之地的船舶可以直达东京开封府。这些改造措施，为城市经济繁荣打下了基础，也基本上奠定了北宋东京城的格局。北宋王朝在此基础上，终于把开封建成了当时的世界名都。

## 第五节　北宋开封，世界东京

公元 960 年，后周的殿前都点检赵匡胤，谎称契丹犯边，率兵北上，在陈桥，也就是现在的河南封丘南，发动兵变，黄袍加身，建立北宋，仍然定都于开封。北宋历经九帝共 168 年，开封一直是王朝的都城。它不仅是当时中国的政治、经济、文化中心，还是当时世界上人口最多、最发达的城市。

作为北宋时的东京城的开封，具有三重城市结构，即皇城、里城和外城。4 条宽阔的御道纵横交错，4 条便利的运河沟通内外，不论达官显贵还是贩夫走卒，在这里都能发现生活的舒适与惬意。皇城位于城市中央，稍微偏向西北，它是三重城中最居中的一重。皇城又名宫城、大内，四周长达 2.5 千米。它的外面砌砖，四角都建有高达数十丈的城楼，以方便瞭望。皇城有 6 座城门，正门面南。城内主要是皇宫和中央政府各机构所在地，建筑极其奢华，雕梁画栋，金碧辉煌。皇城原来是唐代

capital, given the pros and cons of Luoyang and Kaifeng. Shi Jingtang, Emperor Gaozu of the Later Jin Dynasty, renamed the Bianzhou Palace Daning Palace, and proclaimed: "Bianzhou is the capital under the administration of Kaifeng." It was the second time that Kaifeng had been proclaimed capital during the Five Dynasties, but now it was called Dongjing. After spiraling development, it became reinstated as the political center of Kaifeng. After the Later Han Dynasty defeated the Later Jin Dynasty, Kaifeng remained the capital. Its position was retained after the Later Han Dynasty was overcome by the Later Zhou Dynasty. The period of the Five Dynasties extended more than 50 years. Four of the dynasties had selected Kaifeng as their capital for over 40 years. The only exception was the Later Tang Dynasty. In the history of the Five Dynasties, Kaifeng became a new political center in the later period of Chinese feudal society, replacing Chang'an and Luoyang.

In the Later Zhou Dynasty, the political climate was relatively stable and the fortifications of Kaifeng were reinforced. The first step was to build the outer wall, 24,116.5 meters in circumference. The second step was to widen the streets and to dismantle buildings along the streets, to facilitate transportation. The city expansion solved the problems of insufficient construction land and impediments to transportation. Kaifeng developed into a quite admirable city. Chai Rong, the second emperor of the Later Zhou, renovated the waterway by dredging the Bianhe River, which flowed on a straight course through the Huaihe River and into Wuzhang River in the north. Now, vessels coming from Shandong had direct access to Kaifeng. These set the foundation for a prosperous economy and for the institutional pattern of Kaifeng during the Northern Song Dynasty. On that basis, Kaifeng became one of the world's capitals of high renown during the era.

## V. Kaifeng in the Northern Song Dynasty

In 960 AD, General Zhao Kuangyin of the Later Zhou Dynasty falsely accused Khitan of encroaching on Zhou territory. He requested permission to lead troops in retaliation against the north. In Chenqiao (Fengqiu, Henan), he launched a mutiny, proclaimed himself emperor and established the Northern Song Dynasty. During 168 years under the rule of nine emperors of the Northern Song, Kaifeng served as its capital. It was not only the political, economic, and cultural center of China but

节度使的治所，后梁时称为建昌宫，后晋时又改称大宁宫。经考古勘探，目前初步探明皇城的大致范围为：东墙位于今东华门街西侧；西墙北起有线电视塔，向南经杨家湖到原麻刀厂门前；南墙位于今午朝门处的东西一线；北墙位于龙亭大殿北的东线。里城位于皇城与外城之间，原为唐代汴州刺史李勉所筑的汴州城，四周长约 10 077.5 米，共有 10 座城门和两座水门。经考古钻探可知，内城大致为长方形，周长约为 12.5 千米。内城的北墙位于今龙亭大殿北 500 米左右的东西一线，南墙位于今开封城墙大南门瓮城北 350 米左右的东西一线，东墙与西墙与现在开封城墙的东西墙相重叠。外城，又叫新城或罗城，是周世宗柴荣登基后所扩建，周围长约 24 116.5 米。宋神宗时又把其扩展到约 25 082.5 米，并在城墙上建有敌楼，城门外并筑有瓮城。由于外城是东京城的第一道防御屏障，所以在北宋时期，统治者对外城不断加固和扩建。城上四角均建有敌楼，四周筑有马面，城外挖有宽阔的护城河。外城有 12 座城门、6 座水门，除个别城门为直门外，大多数城门是曲门，并且有三重瓮城。经过考古勘探，外城周长达 29 126 米，整体为东西稍短、南北稍长的长方形，与文献记载的大致相符，其四面城墙距离现存的开封城墙 1.5 千米左右。

北宋东京城的街道都是直交，整体看上去像是一个个方格子，非常整齐。主要干线就是四条御道，它们把全城的街道都给串连了起来，非常方便。第一条主干线是从皇宫的正门向南，经过州桥，穿过内城南墙的朱雀门，直到外城的南薰门。第二条主干线是经过州桥向西，先过内城的郑门再到外城的新郑门。第三条主干线是从州桥向东，先过内城的宋门，再到外城的新宋门。第四条主干线是从相国寺前先向东再向北，穿过里城的封丘门，再到外城的新封丘门。全城的大街小巷几乎都能与这四条主干线连接起来，交通非常便捷。

东京的城市管理制度比较先进，与当时的经济社会发展状况相适应。首先是厢坊制度。最上面的一级是开封府，然后是都厢、厢和坊，形成

also the world's most developed city, with the largest population.

Kaifeng had the imperial palace, inner and outer cities in the concentric triple structure, comprised of the palace and the inner and outer cities. Four broad roads crossed the entire city, and four convenient canals were connected inside and outside. People at all levels of life had comfortable and fulfilling lives. The imperial palace was located in the center of the city, slightly to the northwest. The area is also known as Gongcheng (Palace City) or Danei, with a circumference of 2.5 kilometres. The outer side of the palace wall was laid with bricks, and there are dozens of pedestal towers at each corner, for the lookout. There were six gates, one of which faced south. Inside the district, the palace and central government administrations dominated. The buildings were lavishly decorated with sparkling, magnificent carvings and paintings. It was originally in the charge of a governor during the Tang Dynasty, and renamed as Jianchang Palace in the Later Liang Dynasty, and then again, Daning Palace, in the Later Jin Dynasty. Current archaeological excavations prove the rough layout of the imperial palace. The east wall is to the west of Donghuamen Street. The west wall starts from the existing cable TV tower in the north, goes through the Yangjia Lake and finally, ends in the old site of the Madao factory. The south wall is located at the line of Wuchaomen Street; the north wall is located to the east of Longting Hall. The inner city was located between the imperial palace and the outer city. It was originally built by Bianzhou governor Li Mian, during the Tang Dynasty. It was over 10,077.5 meters long. There were ten castle gates and two water gates. According to archaeological survey, the inner city was roughly rectangular, with its perimeter at about 12,500 meters. The north wall of the inner city was about 500 meters from the Longting Hall, while the south wall was 350 meters from the Dananmen Gate. The east and west walls were what are now city walls of Kaifeng. The outer city, also known as the New City or Luo City, was expanded after the emperor of the Later Zhou Dynasty, Chai Rong, was enthroned. It was 24,116.5 meters long in total. The Emperor Shenzong of the Northern Song Dynasty extended it to over 25,082.5 meters, with watchtowers on the walls and barbicans (weng cheng) outside. As the outer city was the first defensive barrier, the rulers in Northern Song continued to strengthen and expand it. Watchtowers were built at the four corners of the city wall, surrounded by defensive towers and a wide moat, encircling. There were twelve city gates and six water gates, most of which were Qumen. Outside were three layers of

完备的四级管理模式。其次是防火与供排水制度。由于坊市紧密结合在一起，店铺多临街开设，与居住区混杂在一起，极易引起火灾，东京开封府为此成立了防火队，一旦出现火情，相关人员能够迅速行动，火灾能够很快被扑灭。在吃水方面，居民主要依靠自家所打的水井，当然开凿水井须经官府批准。在排水方面，城中所挖的水沟是排水的主要力量。每年汛前，官府都会组织人员清淤疏沟，以确保排水通畅。如有阻碍排水的违章建筑，官府通常会进行处理。最后是城市救济与卫生管理制度。官府成立福田院、居养院、安居院等，以安置一些鳏寡孤独之人。官府对街道进行洒水，以保证权贵们出行的卫生。官府严格管理制度，防止侵占公共街道，常在道路两旁立些标志，以确保道路的公共属性。

东京城的制造业比较发达，不仅有小的作坊，还有大的手工工场，主要生产制造船舶、兵器、火药、陶器等。这些行业不仅能工巧匠极多，而且生产分工非常细密，所以产品质量非常优良。东京的商业非常繁荣，堪称当时全国最大的商业城市。当时已出现世界上最早的纸币交子，极大地便利了商业活动。每年向国家交纳的商税数目惊人，已达数十万贯。行会组织大量出现，可见商户数量惊人。贸易场所除了店铺门面之外，还有寺院庙会和都亭馆驿，不仅极大地便利了民众的日常需要，也使对外贸易在官府的管理之下有了固定的交易场所。

东京城的文教事业非常发达。学校众多，有国子监的学校，也有开封府所属的学校。学校设有多种课程，极大地保证了封建统治的人才需要。东京城的藏书机构众多，崇文院是北宋最大的皇家图书馆，所藏图书接近六万卷。这样就为许多大部头的书籍编撰提供了极大的便利，如《太平御览》《太平广记》《册府元龟》《文苑英华》等。私人藏书首推宋敏求，家富藏书三万卷，是东京城最大的私人图书馆。

东京城的文艺娱乐活动丰富多彩。大型的游乐场所也叫瓦子勾栏，里面有说书、杂技、皮影戏、傀儡戏等，还有卖药的、算卦的等。演出

barbicans. Archaeological survey shows that the outer city was shaped in a rectangle of 29,126 meters. It is roughly consistent with recorded documents, that the wall was about 1.5 kilometers far from the existing city wall.

In the Northern Song Dynasty, the streets in Dongjing were straight. From a bird's eye view, the layout appears as uniform squares, of nearly equal dimension. The four main roads linked secondary streets across the city, making for convenient traffic flow. The first main road started at the main entrance of the palace, to the south, went through Zhou bridge and Zhuque Gate of the inner city, until it reached Nanxun Gate of the outer city. The second road went along Zhou Bridge, to the west, passed through Zheng Gate of the inner city and finally reached Xinzheng Gate of the outer city. The third started from Zhou Bridge to the east, went through Song Gate of the inner city, and then reached Xinsong Gate in the outer city. The fourth road started at Xiangguo Temple, first to the east and then to the north, traversed the Fengqiu Gate of the inner city, ended at the Xinfengqiu Gate of the outer city. These four main roads were accessible to all streets of the city so that traffic ran smoothly.

Dongjing's urban management system was relatively advanced, in economic and social development. First, it adopted the Xiangfang system, a hierarchical system. A complete four-level management mode is composed of Kaifeng Prefecture, Duxiang, Xiang and Fang in order of magnitude. The other is the system of fire prevention and water supply and drainage. As workshops and markets were closely built and shops were settled along the residential area, there were considerable risks of fire. A fire brigade was established. As a fire alarm sounded, people were able to respond quickly to bring the fire under control. For water supply, residents drew water from wells they dug themselves. Well-digging required approval from the local authorities. Gutters were dug to control water drainage. Before the annual flood, the government organized work to clear ditches, ensuring smooth drainage. Buildings that impeded drainage normally were demolished by the government. The institution of civic assistance and health management was also set up. Futian Home, the Nursing Home and Anju Home were established by the government to resettle widows, widowers and the childless. The streets were cleaned with water regularly to ensure the sanitation of streets for passing dignitaries. The government maintained strict administration of streets, to ensure that they were not occupied by structures. Signs on both sides of the road proclaimed the streets as public property.

时间从早至晚，民众可以一天都待在里面欣赏节目。最有名的瓦子就是潘楼瓦子和州东、州西瓦子。文化繁荣的基础是良好的经济环境和宽松的政府管理措施，这些是一个城市繁荣发展的基本条件。张择端的《清明上河图》对繁华的东京城作了具体生动的描绘，我们从中可以看到当时的东京城是多么的繁华！当时东京城的人口约 150 万，而同时期的日本京都或朝鲜开城的人口不过才 20 万，巴比伦的人口也不过为 30 万，伦敦的人口居然才只有 1.5 万。美国的《纽约时报》称之为 1 000 年前“世界的中心”。

东京城因北宋而兴，也因北宋而衰。1127 年，金国攻破东京城，尽掳宗室、珍宝而还。北宋亡国后，这座富丽的名都也从此走向了衰落。尽管它也一度成为某些政权的都城，但是毕竟风光不再，逐渐成为一个地方性的中心城市。

## 第六节　金元明清，尽显沧桑

北宋灭亡后，东京城失去了它的首都地位，影响力不复当年。更重要的是，由于宋金战争的影响，汴河长期得不到疏浚，通航能力降低，开封这座依河而兴的城市失去了当年的繁华，迅速走向衰落。

金国统治者把东京改为汴京，这个城市还先后成为两个王朝的首都，一个是张邦昌的大楚政权，另一个是刘豫的大齐政权。不过这两个政权都是金国统治者为了统治原北宋遗民而建立的政权，随着它们的作用减弱，这两个所谓的皇帝也相继被金国统治者撤掉。之后，金国又改汴京为南京，作为国家的陪都。金国统治者完颜亮为了更好地进攻南宋王朝，迁都南京，同时对原北宋皇宫作了一番修建。但是，完颜亮的政策在金国内部引起了激烈的反对，军队哗变，完颜亮死于乱军之中。后继的统治者抛弃了完颜亮大举攻宋的政策，把都城又迁回了燕京，也就是现在

Manufacturing in Kaifeng was advanced, with both small and large workshops. The workshops mainly built ships and made weapons, gunpowder and pottery. A pool of skilled craftsmen and a fine division of production guaranteed good quality products. Trade in Kaifeng was so prosperous that it became the largest commercial city in China. At that time, Jiaozi was the earliest banknote in the world. Jiaozi greatly facilitated commercial activities. The sum of tax collection was astonishing as it reached several hundreds of thousands guan of copper money. The emergence of numerous guilds witnessed the skyrocketing number of merchants. Trade venues such as stores, as well as temples, pavilions and inns met daily needs of the people so that there was established, a fixed trading place under the management of the government.

Culture and education in Kaifeng were well developed. There were institutions like the imperial colleges run by the Directorate of Education, or ones under the administration of Kaifeng Prefecture. A syllabus of courses was designed to meet the demand for talents that served the feudal society. Libraries were abundant in Kaifeng, the largest being the Chongwen Library, the largest royal library of the Northern Song Dynasty. Its collection of books numbered nearly 60,000 volumes. These references greatly facilitated the compilation of many heavy volumes, such as *Overview of Taiping era*, *General Record of Taiping era*, *Ce Fu Yuan Gui* and *Wen Yuan Ying Hua*. The private collector, Song Minqiu, who owned 30,000 books established the largest private library in Kaifeng.

Culture was booming and promoted by regular performances, providing entertainment for the populace. Wazi Goulan was one large entertainment center. Public performances included storytelling, acrobatics, shadow plays and puppet shows. In addition, there were merchants selling medications and geomancers who told fortunes. Performances continued all day, so members of the public could stay and enjoy the shows. The most famous entertainment centers were Panlou Wazi, Zhoudong Wazi and Zhouxi Wazi. The flourishing culture was supported by a healthy economy and an open governmental administration. These elements lay the foundation of prosperous development. Zhang Zeduan's masterpiece, *The Riverside Scene at Qingming Festival*, presented a vivid depiction of the bustling Kaifeng City. What a prosperous city at that time! The population of Dongjing was about 1.5 million. The populations of Tokyo, Japan, or Kaesong, North Korea, were only 200,000, and 300,000 in Babylon, and in London the population was only 15,000. *The New York*

的北京。这种局面一直到金国末年，由于蒙古统治者的军事压迫，金国统治者不得不又一次迁都开封，直到金亡。蒙古人攻打了开封一年左右才破城，可见开封军民团结一心抵抗外敌的意志。按照蒙古军的惯例，如遇抵抗，城破后一律屠城。可是，或许开封人团结御敌的精神震动了蒙古人，或许开封的能工巧匠太多，对蒙古人还有利用价值，蒙古人最终没有屠城，这个古都逃过了一劫。

金国统治时期，对开封做了一定程度的修缮，主要是对里城的修复，将里城的南、北墙加以外扩，东、西墙还是沿用北宋时期的城墙，只是稍微加高而已。同时，为了抵御蒙古，对开封的城楼、护城河等都做了整修，并塞住了 4 座城门，以防蒙古军大举攻城。整体来说，金人没有对开封城做较大的修缮，只是因地制宜，足够使用而已，这也是由当时的形势所决定的。金人将首都南迁，政治上已是落了下风，经济上千疮百孔，军事上更是捉襟见肘，也只能大致利用原来的城池为自己安身保命而已。

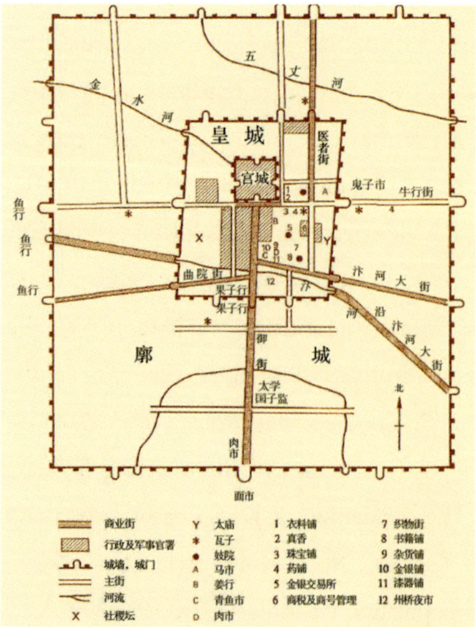


北宋东京城示意图

Dongjing City of the Northern Song Dynasty

*Times* has described Dongjing as the center of the world of 1,000 years ago.

Dongjing would be revived and then collapse, as the Northern Song Dynasty rose and fell. In 1127 AD, the Jin Dynasty overran Dongjing and looted the treasures of the imperial clans. After the fall of the Northern Song Dynasty, the city entered terminal decline. Although it had served as the capital of great kingdoms, its status gradually was depleted, until it became a regional center.

## VI. The Decline of Dongjing in the Jin, Yuan, Ming and Qing Dynasties

After the fall of the Northern Song Dynasty, Dongjing City lost its central place and influence of earlier times. More importantly, the Song-Jin War interrupted the dredging of the Bianhe River, leaving a reduced capacity for river traffic. Prosperity slipped away and Kaifeng lost its place as the paragon of Chinese cities.

The rulers of the Jin Dynasty changed the name of the capital to Bianjing, which remained capital for two succeeding dynasties. Zhang Bangchang's Dachu regime and Liu Yu's Daqi regime were created to control the Northern Song people. These so-called "emperors" were deposed by the Jin rulers, who considered these minor commanders to be of no value. Later, Jin changed the name of Bianjing to Nanjing, declaring it to be a temporary capital. In order to mount a fierce attack on the Southern Song Dynasty, the Jin ruler, Wanyan Liang moved to Nanjing and renovated the former imperial palace of the Northern Song Dynasty. The policy of Wanyan Liang, however, aroused fierce opposition and precipitated a mutiny by the military that cost Wanyan Liang's life. Wanyan Liang's successor cancelled Wanyan Liang's plans for a massive attack on Song and returned to Yanjing, which is now Beijing. The military oppression of the Mongolian rulers forced the Jin ruler to retreat to Kaifeng, where he remained until Jin fell. The Mongolians attacked Kaifeng for almost a year before breaking the city defenses. The resistance showed the willingness of the army and the people of Kaifeng to resist enemies. It had been a practice adapted by the Mongolian leaders to destroy any city that resisted the Mongolian advance. Possibly the Mongolians were impressed by the unity and determination of the people in their resistance to aggressors, and thus decided to spare the city from destruction.

During the reign of Jin, Kaifeng was reconstructed to a certain extent. In the

现在我们经过考古钻探得知，金人对开封城的建设还是在北宋东京城的基础上加以整修，整个城市的格局没有变化，城门、街道的位置也没有变化。当时的里城南墙向外扩了350米，到达今天的大南门；北墙也向外扩了700多米，达到今天开封城墙的北墙处。

有趣的是，金人即使在亡国之前，仍然没有停止科举取士这项工作。开封市博物馆现藏有一碑，即《女真进士题名碑》，它是金哀宗正大元年（1224）六月十五日所立，系用女真小字书写。

元朝时，在开封设南京路，后改为汴梁路。实行行省制度后，开封是河南、江北等行中书省的省会，这是开封为河南省会的开端。元朝汴梁城仍然保持了金朝南京城的格局，只是对局部进行过两次整修，分别是在元世祖年间和元仁宗年间。元末红巾军起义，汴梁的元军守将把许多城门塞住，以防红巾军攻城，只留了5座城门以供出入。

元朝初年，由于蒙古人重视畜牧业，开封周围的农田都被改为牧场，黄河也已改道，离开封较近，开封的经济社会发展受到了严重的制约。后来，统治者改变了政策，下令散居在各地的回族炮手都定居在汴梁，以农业为生。这样，开封在汉回各族群众的努力下，逐渐恢复了生机，经济迅速发展起来。意大利人马可·波罗在其游记中回忆，开封人民以经商、手艺为生，都很富裕。可见，这时的开封城已经比较繁华了。元朝末年，黄河水患极其严重，总治河防使贾鲁征发兵民17万，全面治理黄河，同时疏导蔡河故道，恢复其航运功能，使江南的物资可以运抵开封，故而蔡河后又叫贾鲁河。

元朝时，统治者在汴梁城修建了大元朝万寿宫，以纪念全真教的创教始祖王喆，这就是今天的延庆观，后来不幸毁于战火，现仅存玉皇阁斋堂，其造型独特，全国罕见，现在已是全国重点文物保护单位。

明初，朱元璋在攻下开封后，把元朝时的名字汴梁路改为开封府，定为北京。由于开封的陪都地位，明初统治者大力整修开封，外城已经

inner city, the south and north walls were expanded. The east and west walls were raised slightly, without substantial renovation. The towers and moats were renovated and four of the gates were blocked, to guard against the Mongolian invasion. On the whole, there was no substantial renovation in Kaifeng, only what was necessary, in light of local conditions. It was only because of the decline of its political stability, economy and military power in that era, that the Jin moved to the south and temporarily settled in Kaifeng, as a refuge.

Archaeological survey shows that Kaifeng was renovated by the Jin based on Dongjing of the Northern Song Dynasty. The layout of the entire city and the location of the city gates remained the same. The south wall of the inner city was expanded outwards, by 350 meters to the position of what is now the Great South Gate. The north wall also was moved out, by over 700 meters, to what has become the north wall.

Interestingly, the Jin insisted on organizing imperial examinations, even as the city was on the verge of collapse. The Kaifeng City Museum now holds a stone tablet of *Jurchen Jinshi Recipients*, written in Jurchen inscription. The tablet dates back to the reign of Emperor Aizong of the Jin Dynasty.

In the Yuan Dynasty, Nanjing Prefecture was built around Kaifeng. The name was changed later, to Bianliang Prefecture. After the implementation of the provincial system, Kaifeng became the provincial capital of the northern regions of Henan. It was on that foundation that Kaifeng was to emerge, as the provincial capital of Henan. Bianliang City of the Yuan Dynasty remained much the same as the Nanjing City of the Jin Dynasty. Bianling City underwent two partial repairs, respectively during the Emperor Shizu and Emperor Renzong of the Yuan Dynasty years. In the uprising of the Red Scarf Army at the end of the Yuan era, the Yuan generals blocked most of Bianliang's gates to forestall attack from the Red Scarf. Only five accessible gates remained.

In the early years of the Yuan Dynasty, the Mongolians gave priority to animal husbandry. Harvested land was converted to pasture land. The course of the Yellow River changed, bringing it close to Kaifeng, where there were severe constraints already affecting economic and social development. Later, the rulers changed their policies and called for Hui gunners scattered around the country to settle in Bianliang and make a living by pursuing agriculture. With the efforts of Han and

毁于战火，所以把原为土城的里城修为砖城，这就是开封城墙的前身。10年之后，开封的陪都地位被取消，因为此时朱元璋已经放弃了在开封建都的想法。他把吴王改封为周王，令其就藩开封。靖难之役时，周王大力支持朱棣，明成祖即位后，对周王恩赏有加。故有明一代，周王地位特别显赫，王府也比其他藩王的壮丽。明代开封势若两京，政治、经济地位都非常高。

明末，李自成起义军攻打开封，末代周王串通官兵挖开了黄河大堤，想水淹起义军。谁知弄巧成拙，义军远避高处，开封地势较低，竟然成了一片泽国，城中37万多人，幸存者不到3万人。这是开封第二次遭受灭顶之灾。一代名城，繁华不再矣。

清初，开封城内人烟稀少，一片黄沙，荒凉无比。康熙元年（1662），统治者重修开封城，城墙和城门都在原来位置。当时城内有许多空地和水泊，现在的潘家湖、杨家湖和包公湖就是在这时掘土成湖的。城内生意渐起，人口也慢慢增多。可惜的是，道光二十一年，也就是公元1841年，这年的六月，黄河决于张湾，开封又一次被黄河水淹没了。这是开封遭受的第三次灭顶之灾。水退后，统治者又重新修筑开封城，这就是今天的开封城。

清末，汴洛铁路修成，开封经济有了一定的发展。辛亥革命后，冯玉祥主政河南，比较注意城市建设，加宽了中山路，城市面貌略为改观。

## 第七节 古都开封历史名人轶事

开封名人辈出，人文遗迹众多，在这片古老的土地上发生过许多令人叹为观止的故事，涌现出诸多令人景仰的伟大人物，如魏惠王开凿鸿沟、信陵君窃符救赵、蔡邕巧造焦尾琴、祖逖击楫中流、宋太祖陈桥兵变等。

Hui, Kaifeng gradually recovered its vitality. The city's economy and society recovered quickly and flourished. The Italian Marco Polo, in his travel log, recalled that the people of Kaifeng were rich in business and crafts. It can be seen easily that Kaifeng was quite prosperous at the time. At the close of the Yuan Dynasty, the annual flood of the Yellow River began to create havoc in the city. An official, Jia Lu, recruited 170,000 militia to bring the flood under control and clear the Caihe River course, to restore shipping from the south to Kaifeng. Later the river was called the Jialu River.

In the Yuan Dynasty, rulers built the Wanshou Palace in Bianliang, in memory of the founding father of the Quanzhen Sect, Wang Zhe. The palace later became known as the Yanqing Taoist Temple. The temple was razed by fire in a later war. Only the Hall of the Jade Emperor was spared. Owing to the uniqueness of its construction, the Hall of the Jade Emperor is acknowledged as a key national cultural edifice.

At the beginning of the Ming Dynasty, Zhu Yuanzhang changed the name Bianliang Prefecture to Kaifeng Prefecture, and set Beijing as its capital. At the temporary capital of Kaifeng, rulers of the early Ming Dynasty restored the city with considerable efforts. The outer city wall was destroyed in the war, so the inner city wall was rebuilt with bricks, to become the predecessor of the present day Kaifeng city wall. Ten years later, Kaifeng ended its role as a temporary capital. Zhu Yuanzhang already had rejected the establishment of a capital at Kaifeng. King Wu was given the new title of King Zhou and ordered to establish a tributary state in Kaifeng. Later, King Zhou gave strong support to Zhu Di in the Jingnan campaign, who repaid him with lavish awards after Zhu Di ascended the throne. Therefore, King Zhou rose to particular prominence. His palace was more magnificent than any other. During the Ming Dynasty, the political climate and economy of Kaifeng were as important as those of the capital.

At the close of the Ming Dynasty, when Li Zicheng of the Rebellion attacked Kaifeng, King Zhou worked with the army to open the Yellow River levee and drown the rebels. The rebels escaped to high ground, unexpectedly but Kaifeng was swamped, situated as it was on low ground. Fewer than 30,000 of 370,000 civilians survived the flood. It was the second time that Kaifeng had been devastated by floodwaters. A city with a proud history was left in ruins.

At the beginning of the Qing Dynasty, Kaifeng lay in desolation. In the first year of Emperor Kangxi, Kaifeng was rebuilt on its former site, without change to

## 1. 魏惠王开凿鸿沟

魏惠王是有史明确记载的第一个在开封定都的国君，对开封的发展有着巨大的历史贡献。魏惠王还有一大功绩，就是开挖鸿沟。公元前361年，为了战争需要，魏惠王曾两次大兴水利，开挖鸿沟。鸿沟西自荥阳引黄河水为源，向东流经中牟、开封，折而南下，入颍河通淮河，把黄河与淮河之间的济、濮、汴、睢、颍、涡、汝、泗、菏等主要河道连接起来，构成鸿沟水系。鸿沟水量充沛，与其相连的河道，水位相对稳定，对发展航运很有利。它向南通淮河、邗沟，与长江贯通；向东通济水、泗水；向北通黄河，溯黄河西向，与洛河、渭水相连，使河南成为全国水路交通的核心地区。鸿沟的开凿，为后来京杭大运河的开凿创造了条件。

楚汉相争时，曾以鸿沟为界平分天下划定两国疆域。我们现在仍在玩的象棋，两军对垒的分割线“楚河汉界”就是鸿沟。魏惠王迁都大梁后，他所修筑的大梁坚城，奠定了今日开封城的基础；他所开凿的人工运河鸿沟，使开封城四周水道畅达，景象万千，颇具名都气象。时至今日，开封仍以多水而著称于世，享有“北方水城”的美誉。

## 2. 蔡邕巧造焦尾琴

东汉时期的蔡邕是陈留郡圉县（今河南省开封市圉镇）人，他精通音律，才华横溢，能于琴声中听出杀音，令弹琴的人与听琴的人都佩服不已。相传，蔡邕在吴地（今江浙一带）时，曾偶然听到一块桐木在火中爆裂的声音，知道这是一块好木材，因此赶快把它抢救出来。他依据木头的长短、形状，制成一张七弦琴，音色非常美妙，由于此琴的尾部

the original position of its walls and gates. There were many open areas and lakes, where Panjia Lake, Yangjia Lake and Baogong Lake had formed. As business in the city rebounded, the population gradually increased. Then, disaster struck again, in June, 1841, when the levees broke at Zhangwan Bay, and for a third time, Kaifeng was flooded by the Yellow River. When the water receded, the ruler rebuilt the city again, the city that grew into modern Kaifeng.

At the end of the Qing Dynasty, the Bian-Luo railway was built, promoting great economic development. After the Revolution of 1911 AD, Feng Yuxiang, who took charge of Henan, improved the urban infrastructure, including expanding Zhongshan Road.

## VII. The Famous Historical Figures in Ancient Kaifeng

Numerous cultural relics have been retained in Kaifeng, bearing witness to the numerous historical events and notable individuals dotting the history of the city. Among the most memorable were King Hui's excavation of Honggou channel, Lord Xinling's theft of the imperial seal which helped to preserve the Zhao, Cai Yong's skilled Qin-making, Zu Ti's tapping the barge in the midstream and Emperor Taizu's coup at Chenqiao.

**1. King Hui's excavation of Honggou channel**

King Hui of Wei, was the first monarch who founded the capital at Kaifeng in recorded history. He made great contributions to the development of the city. King Hui also made important strides in the excavation of the Honggou channel. In 361 BC, he launched two water resources projects, in support of Kaifeng's military needs. The source of the channel was the Yellow River, in the west of Xingyang City. The man-made channel flowed eastward to Zhongmou and Kaifeng, and then southward through the Yinghe River into the Huaihe River. A water system was created, connecting the Ji, Pu, Bian, Sui, Ying, Guo, Ru, Si and He rivers. Water was abundant in the channel, and the water level of the connected waterways was relatively stable, which provided substantial benefit to shipping. The channel was cut in a southerly direction, through the Huaihe River and the Hangou River and on to the Yangzi River. The channel flowed eastward to the Jishui and Sishui River. To the north, it passed through the Yellow River, connected with the Luohe and Weishui rivers. Therefore, Henan became the

有烧焦过的印迹，所以人们叫它焦尾琴。“焦尾”以它悦耳的音色和特有的制法闻名四海，和齐桓公的“号钟”、楚庄王的“绕梁”、司马相如的“绿绮”并称为中国古代“四大名琴”。

### 3. 信陵君窃符救赵

信陵君（？—前243），魏昭王少子，即魏无忌，号信陵君，战国时期魏国（都城大梁，今开封）著名的军事家。因安厘王元年（公元前276年）被封于信陵（今河南宁陵县），所以后世皆称其为信陵君，与春申君黄歇、孟尝君田文、平原君赵胜并称“战国四公子”。他为人仁爱宽厚、礼贤下士，士人因而争相前往归附于他，最高峰时门下曾有3 000名食客。所以当时的魏无忌威名远扬，各诸侯国连续多年都不敢动兵侵犯魏国。司马迁的《史记·魏公子列传》记载了著名的“信陵君窃符救赵”的故事，列传中147处使用“公子”来称呼信陵君，这在另外战国三公子的列传中是没有的。

### 4. 祖逖击楫中流

祖逖是两晋时期的人，西晋灭亡后，他奉东晋元帝之命率部北伐。北渡长江，船至中流之时，他眼望面前滚滚东去的江水，感慨万千，想到山河破碎和生灵涂炭的情景，想到困难的处境和壮志难伸的愤懑，豪气干云，热血涌动，敲着船楫朗声发誓：“祖逖不能清中原而复济者，有如大江！”意思是若不能平定中原，收复失地，自己就像这大江一样有去无回！后人便用“中流击楫”比喻立志奋发图强。祖逖一片热血报国的壮志永远被后人铭记。

core of the national waterway system. The excavation of Honggou channel created conditions for the subsequent excavation of the North and South Grand Canal.

During the Clash between the Chu and Han, the channel was established as the border between the two regimes. This historical fact is reflected in the Chinese chess board. The battle line in the middle of the board represents the frontier between the Chu and Han. After King Hui of Wei moved to Daliang, the rebuilt, solid city laid the foundation for modern Kaifeng. The artificial canal linked waterways around a city surrounded by natural beauty. Today Kaifeng is renowned for its waterways, enjoying its nickname of "Water City in Northern China".

**2. Cai Yong's skilled Qin-making**

In the Eastern Han Dynasty, Cai Yong lived in Yu County of Chenliu Prefecture, now called Yu County of Kaifeng, Henan Province. He was proficient in the playing of chords and rhythms. It was said that he could read the thoughts of the musician from the sound made by the strings, to the amazement of the players and their listeners. According to the legend, Cai Yong in the Wu (now in Jiangsu and Zhejiang), came upon a fine piece of paulownia wood, burning in a fire. He rescued the wood and built a heptachord based on the length and shape of the wood. The instrument produced beautiful tones. Owing to a burn mark that remained in the wood, the seven-string musical instrument was called Jiaowei Qin. The instrument was famed for its beautiful sound and unique Qin-making. It is regarded as one of ancient China's Four Heptachords, along with Duke Huan's Haozhong, King Zhuang's Raoliang and Sima Xiangru's Lvyi.

**3. Lord Xinling, Legendary Hero of the Warring States**

Lord Xinling(?-243 BC) was born as Wei Wuji, the son of King Zhao of Wei. He was a famed militarist of Wei (Whose capital was Daliang, today's Kaifeng), during the Warring States Period. He was called Lord Xinling by later generations. His title was conferred in Xinling, (now Ningling County, Henan Province), during the first year of King Anli ( 276 BC). Lord Xinling was known as one of the Four Lords of the Warring States Period, along with Lord Chunshen of Chu (Huang Xie), Lord Mengchang of Qi (Tian Wen) and Lord Pingyuan of Zhao (Zhao Sheng). Lord Xinling was reputed to have been generous and courteous, a man with a large following. At their acme, his followers were said to number up to 3,000. His reputation discouraged vassal states from invading Wei for over a decade. Sima Qian's

## 5. 宋太祖陈桥兵变

“陈桥兵变”是宋太祖赵匡胤发动的取代后周建立宋朝的兵变事件。959 年，周世宗柴荣崩，7 岁的周恭帝柴宗训即位，殿前都点检、归德军节度使赵匡胤与禁军高级将领石守信、王审琦等掌握了军权。

960年正月初一，传闻契丹联合北汉南下攻周，宰相范质等未辨真伪，急遣赵匡胤统率诸军北上御敌。周军行至陈桥驿，赵匡胤和赵普等密谋，发动兵变，众将将黄袍盖在赵匡胤身上，拥立他为皇帝。随后，赵匡胤率军回师开封，京城守将石守信、王审琦开城迎接赵匡胤入城，胁迫周恭帝禅位。赵匡胤即位后，改国号为“宋”，仍定都开封。这一故事又称“黄袍加身”。

work, *Shi Ji—Lords of Wei*, records the legend of Lord Xinling's saving Zhao by stealing the imperial seal. In the story, "lord" was used 147 times, with reference to Lord Xinling.

**4. Zu Ti's tapping the bow of boat in the midstream**

Zu Ti, a native of the Eastern and Western Jin, was ordered by the Emperor Yuan of the Eastern Jin to expand the empire northward, after the fall of the Western Jin. As he travelled north, toward the Yangtze River, upon reaching the midstream of the river, he was filled with regret to discover its eastward current. Recalling the destruction of his country and the misery of its surviving people, he tapped the bow of his boat with paddle and swore: "I commit to regaining the lost land, by clearing the Central Plains! It's as the river flows." His pledge is interpreted to mean that like the flowing water, he never would return, if he failed in his pledge to regain the lost territory of the Central Plains. The phrase is often used in pledging determined efforts to achieve a goal. It will be remembered by future generations that Zu Ti dedicated his life to the service of his country.

**5. Zhao Kuangyin's Coup at Chenqiao**

The coup at Chenqiao was initiated by Zhao Kuangyin (the Emperor Taizu of Song), who dealt the fatal blow that struck down the Later Zhou Dynasty. In 959 AD, the seven-year-old Chai Zongxun, the Emperor Gong of the Later Zhou, took the throne, after the death of Chai Rong, also known by his temple name Shizong. General Zhao Kuangyin shared military power with the palace guard commanders of Shi Shouxin and Wang Shenqi.

On the first day of the lunar new year in 960 AD, rumors spread that Khitan and the Northern Han had attacked the Zhou. Fan Zhi, the chancellor of the Later Zhou, was uncertain about the reliability of the news and ordered Zhao Kuangyin, urgently, to amass troops and march north to mount resistance. As the army arrived at Chenqiao, Zhao Kuangyin and Zhao Pu conspired to mutiny. Zhao Kuangyin wore an imperial robe, alongside the other generals. He was acclaimed as the new emperor. Subsequently, Zhao Kuangyin led the army back to Kaifeng, and the generals of the city defence, Shi Shouxin and Wang Shenqi opened the city gate, to welcome him back. The Emperor Gong of the Later Zhou was forced to abdicate the throne in favour of Zhao Kuangyin. Thereafter, the dynasty was given the name "Song". Its capital was set in Kaifeng. The legend that recounts this tale is, "Huang Pao Jia Shen", or acclaiming an emperor with the imperial yellow robe by one's supporters.

# 第三章

# 七朝古都——安阳

# Chapter Ⅲ

# Anyang: The Ancient Capital of Seven Dynasties

安阳是河南的一个省辖市，位于河南省最北部，地处山西、河北、河南三省交会处，西倚太行山，东连华北平原，北邻邯郸，南接鹤壁、新乡。在漫长的中国历史上，先后有商、曹魏、后赵、冉魏、前燕、东魏、北齐等7个王朝在这里建都。商代的都城称为“殷”，其他6个王朝时的安阳通常被称为“邺”，因此安阳又简称殷或邺。

安阳是中国著名的古都之一，国家历史文化名城，华夏文明的中心之一。之所以有此美誉，是因为安阳是甲骨文的最早发现地，也是《周易》的发源地。与此同时，安阳殷墟也是世界公认的、当今中国所能确定的商代最早都城遗址，有“洹水帝都”“殷商故都”“文字之都”的美誉。

## 第一节　盘庚迁殷，开启繁荣

根据史书的记载，商朝最初建都的地方并不是现在的安阳。当商部族还处于部落时期时，一直过着游牧的生活，主要活动在黄河中下游地区。商汤建国之前，商部族曾经迁徙过8次，商汤建国之后到盘庚定都殷墟又迁移了5次。

商汤建立商朝后，商朝出现了多次内乱，政治腐败，贵族奢侈，王室政治斗争激烈，阶级矛盾尖锐，加上频繁的天灾，到商王盘庚即位的时候，商王朝的统治已经岌岌可危。为了缓和阶级矛盾，挽救王朝的命运，盘庚决定放弃原来的都城，迁徙到北蒙，又称为殷，即今天的安阳。当时的殷地并不富裕，也没有太多的人口，可以说是一片荒芜。但是这里有洹水环绕，水资源丰沛，取水便利，又有洹水定期泛滥带来大量肥沃的土地，于是统治者选定了这里作为迁徙的目的地。

为了完成迁都的大业，盘庚做了大量的工作，他劝告贵族，说明迁都的必要性和紧迫性，鼓励民众不怕吃苦。在盘庚的不懈努力下，迁都最终获得了成功。从公元前1318年商王盘庚把都城迁移至殷地，到公元前1046年商王帝辛亡国，商代的国都一直没再改变过。商王朝在这

Anyang, a provincially governed city in Henan, is located in the northernmost part of Henan and at the intersection of Shanxi, Hebei and Henan provinces with Taihang Mountain in the west, the North China Plain in the east, Handan in the north, and Hebi and Xinxiang in the south. In the long history of China, there were seven dynasties (the Shang, Cao Wei, Later Zhao, Ran Wei, Qian Yan, Eastern Wei and Northern Qi danasties) which established their capitals in Anyang successively. The capital of the Shang Dynasty was called "Yin". In the other six dynasties, their capitals were often called "Ye", so Anyang is also called Yin or Ye.

Anyang is one of China's famous ancient capitals, a national historical and cultural city, and one of the centers of Chinese civilization. The reason for this reputation is that Anyang was the earliest place that discovered the Oracle, and was the birthplace of *The Book of Changes*. At the same time, Anyang or Yin Ruins is also universally recognized as the earliest capital of the Shang Dynasty, which can be identified in today's China. It has a good reputation of "Huanshui Emperor Capital", "Ancient Capital of Yin and Shang" and "Capital of Chinese Characters".

## I. Pangeng: Moving the Shang Capital to Yin

According to the history books, the place where the Shang Dynasty originally built its capital was not where Anyang is located today. When the Shang tribe was still in the tribal period, they lived a nomadic life, mainly in the middle and lower reaches of the Yellow River. Before the founding of the Shang Dynasty, the Shang tribe had moved to other places eight times. After Shang Tang founded the Shang Dynasty, the capital moved five times until King Pangeng built the capital in Yin Ruins (modern Anyang).

After Shang Tang founded the Shang Dynasty, the country experienced a series of civil strife, political corruption, aristocratic luxury, fierce political struggles in the royal family, sharp class contradictions, and frequent natural disasters. These societal struggles made the rule of the Shang Dynasty less efficient and effective until Pangeng was on the throne. In order to ease class contradictions and save the dynasty's destiny, Pangeng decided to abandon the original capital and migrate to Beimeng, also known as Yin, which is today's Anyang. At that time Beimeng was not rich, and there was no large population there. It could be said to be a wasteland. But it was surrounded by Huan water. Abundant water resources, convenient water intake, and the regular irrigation brought

里经历了盘庚、小辛、小乙、武丁、祖庚、祖甲、廪辛、康丁、武乙、文丁、帝乙、帝辛共8代12位国王273年的统治，殷一直是中国商代后期的政治、经济、文化、军事中心。因此，商朝又称为殷商。

如果说盘庚迁殷开启了商朝繁荣的大门，那么商王武丁则实现了商朝的空前强大。武丁是商王盘庚的侄子，是商王小乙的儿子。相传，武丁在少年时期，他的父亲就派他到宫廷之外和平民一起劳动，因此，他了解到很多民众的疾苦和生活的艰辛，与下层群众非常接近。当他继任君主之后，一心想要复兴商朝，但是缺少得力的大臣来辅佐，于是他到处在民间寻找治国的人才。他先是寻访到了既懂得政治又懂得军事的甘盘，后来又找到了刑徒出身的贤人傅说，让甘盘和傅说担任宰相之职，推行改革，使得商朝的政治、军事力量不断增强，国土面积更为广阔。

关于武丁寻访傅说还有一段有趣的故事。武丁继位之后想要完成商朝复兴的大业，但没有得力的大臣，武丁非常郁闷，三年没有说一句话。有一天夜晚武丁做梦遇到一个圣人，名叫说，他就按照梦中见到的样貌观察群臣百官，但发现都不是在梦中所见之人。于是武丁派人到各处寻找，终于在一个叫傅险的地方找到了说。当时说正在服刑，在傅险筑路，于是大臣把他带来见武丁，武丁通过观察和谈话，确定了这正是他梦中之人，并任命他为宰相。后来，傅说把商朝治理得非常繁荣。

武丁在位时期在政治上取得了非凡的成绩。他把很多新开辟的领土，或直接封给征伐的将领，或封给当地臣服的氏族、方国的首领。当时臣服于商的氏族、方国有90多个，他们不仅有纳贡的义务，还要经常奉命征伐。武丁还通过与地方首领的联姻，或娶诸侯之女为妃，或将王室之女嫁于诸侯等，来加强与诸侯国的联系，增强了国家统治的力度。武丁还在征服的地区建造了城邑，开展武装殖民，大大加强了对新的疆域的统治。当时，商四周的氏族、方国不少还处于原始落后的游牧生活阶段，武丁的行为实际上是在这些地区播撒了文明的种子。

武丁在军事上也做出了巨大的贡献。针对朔方、土方等经常侵扰商

fertile soil. So the rulers chose Beimeng as a destination for migration.

In order to relocate the capital, Pangeng did a lot of work. He explained to the nobility the necessity and urgency of relocating the capital and encouraged people to take pains and work hard to relocate the capital. With King Pangeng's unremitting persistence, he successfully relocated the capital. Since 1318 BC when King Pangeng moved the capital to the land of Yin, the capital of the Shang Dynasty was not changed until 1046 BC when the Shang Dynasty was conquered. The Shang Dynasty experienced a 273-year rule of these 12 kings: Pangeng, Xiaoxin, Xiaoyi, Wuding, Zugeng, Zujia, Linxin, Kangding, Wuyi, Wending, Diyi and Dixin. The capital Yin had always been the political, economic, cultural and military centers of the late Shang Dynasty in China. Therefore, the Shang Dynasty is also known as Yin Shang.

If King Pangeng's moving to Yin can be seen as the start of the prosperity of the Shang Dynasty, then King Wuding made the Shang Dynasty unprecedentedly powerful. Wuding was the nephew of King Pangeng, the son of King Xiaoyi. According to legend, when Wuding was a teenager, he was sent by his father to work with common people outside the palace. Because he worked with the common people, he knew about people's sufferings and hardships. He was very close to the lower classes. When Wuding succeeded the throne, he decided to revive the Shang Dynasty. However, there was a lack of competent ministers. He searched everywhere for talents to run the country. He first searched Gan Pan, who mastered both politics and military. Later, he found the sage Fu Yue, who had been a criminal. He let Gan Pan and Fu Yue be the prime ministers and appointed them to implement reforms, which enhanced the power of politics and the military of the Shang Dynasty and widened the land.

There is an interesting story about Wuding's search for Fu Yue. After Wuding succeeded to the throne, he wanted to revive the Shang Dynasty. But he had no competent minister to assist him. He was very depressed, and did not say a word in three years. One day, Wuding dreamed of encountering a saint who was called Yue. He observed the officials according to the appearance he saw in his dream, but found no one. So Wuding sent people to look around and finally found Yue in a place called Fuxian. At that time, Yue was serving his sentence and building a road at Fuxian. Yue was brought to Wuding. Through observation and conversation Wuding confirmed that Yue was the person in his dream. He appointed Yue to be the Prime Minister. Later, with the governance of Fu Yue, the Shang Dynasty became very prosperous.

朝边地和属国，甚至联合威胁商朝西北边境安全的形势，武丁采取各个击破的办法，多次带兵进攻，最终征服了朔方和土方。他又用 3 年时间平定了鬼方，击败了羌方。他还统兵南征，深入荆楚一带，击败荆楚军，出兵征伐夷方、巴方、蜀及虎方等。

武丁在政治和军事上的得力举措，使得商朝国力强盛。司马迁在《史记》中称赞武丁说，武丁推行德政，政治清明，深得天下民众拥戴，商朝得以复兴，所以被尊为殷高宗。

武丁是一位成功的政治家、军事家，他的功绩与他的妻子妇好是分不开的。妇好是我国历史上第一位有文字记载的女将军，她也是第 23 代商王武丁的妻子之一。妇好并不姓妇，妇好的父姓是一个“亚”形中画“兕”形的标志。妇好嫁给武丁之后，武丁给了她相当丰厚的封土和民众。在她的封地上，她得到了“好”的氏名，被尊称为“妇好”。甲骨文中有关她的记载有 200 余条，商王朝的后人们尊称她为“母辛”“妣辛”“后母辛”等。

妇好

Fu Hao

During the reign of King Wuding, he made extraordinary achievements in politics. He gave many of the new territories directly either to the generals or leaders of local clans and states that have been conquered. At that time, more than 90 clans and states were subject to the Shang Dynasty. They were not only obliged to pay tribute but also summoned to fight. Wuding also strengthened the ties with the vassal states to increase the rule of states through the marriage with local leaders or the vassal states. Wuding also built settlements in the conquered areas, conducted armed colonization, and greatly strengthened the rule of the new territories. At that time, many of the clans and states around the Shang Dynasty were still in the primitive and backward period of nomadic life. Wuding's behavior actually sowed the seeds of civilization in these areas.

Wuding also made tremendous contributions to the military. In response to the frequent intrusion of Shuofang and Tufang on the border and vassal states of the Shang Dynasty, and even the joint threat to the security of the northwest border of the Shang Dynasty, Wuding took various measures. He led his troops to attack his enemies many times, and eventually defeated the Shuofang and Tufang in battle. Then Wuding spent another three years defeating the armies of Guifang and Qiangfang. He also led the army to march south, and he went deep into the area of Jingchu and defeated the Jingchu army. He sent the troops to fight against Yifang, Bafang, Shu and Hufang.

Due to Wuding's effective political and military measures, the Shang Dynasty became powerful. Sima Qian praised Wuding in the book *Shi Ji* (*Records of the Grand Historian*): Wuding advocated to rule the country with virtue and won the support of people, which revived the Shang Dynasty. Wuding was honored as Emperor Gaozong of Yin.

Wuding was a successful politician and military strategist. His achievements were inseparable from his wife Fu Hao. Fu Hao was the first female general to be recorded in the Chinese history, and she was also one of the wives of Wuding, the 23rd King of Shang. Fu was not Fu Hao's surname. Her surname was a symbol of a sub-shaped Chinese painting. After getting married to Wuding, Fu Hao gained quite a lot of fiefdoms and people. On her land, she got the name "Hao" which means "good", which was why she was honored as Fu Hao. There are more than 200 records about her in the oracle bones. The future generations of the Shang Dynasty respected her as "Mother Xin", "Bi Xin" and "Houmu Xin".

Fu Hao was the daughter of a tribal leader. She was smart, beautiful, brave, familiar

妇好是一位部落首领的女儿，聪明美貌，通晓兵事，骁勇善战。嫁给武丁后的某一年，商王朝北方边境遭到敌方入侵，派去征讨的将领迟迟不能取胜，在此情况下，妇好主动请战，要求率兵前往助战。武丁犹豫不决，担心妻子不能胜任，最后以占卜求吉凶，显示大吉之兆，于是妇好被任命为大将军。到达前线后，妇好指挥调度有方，战争打响，身先士卒，与士兵同甘共苦，很快就击败了敌人，取得了胜利。从此以后，武丁对妇好刮目相看，常把国家军事委托于她。妇好先后率领军队击败了北边的土方和南边的夷国、巴方、鬼方等 20 多个小国。其中，在对羌方的一次战役中，武丁将王朝一半以上的兵力，大约 13 000 余人，都交给她指挥。妇好没有辜负武丁的重托，经过一次激烈的战斗之后，取得了决定性的胜利，解决了多年来商王朝西北边境的战乱骚扰，使敌人归顺降服。史学家认为，此战的意义不亚于传说中的黄帝与蚩尤之战，其对于殷商王朝乃至整个中华民族的历史，都具有伟大的划时代意义。

1976 年，考古人员在安阳西郊小屯村北发现了妇好的陵墓。该墓

殷墟

Yin Ruins

with military affairs, and good at fighting. One year after marrying Wuding, Fu Hao found that the northern border of the Shang Dynasty was invaded by enemy forces. The generals and soldiers that were sent to the war were unable to win in battle, so Fu Hao took the initiative and asked to lead the soldiers into battle against the enemy. Wuding hesitated and worried that his wife could be incompetent. He sought for good and bad fortune by divination, which revealed good fortune if his wife led the soldiers into battle. So Wuding appointed Fu Hao as the general. After arriving at the front line, Fu Hao commanded and led her troops in a good way. When the war started, she took the lead and shared joys and sorrows with soldiers. She quickly defeated the enemy and won the war. From then on, Wuding was impressed with Fu Hao and often entrusted the national military to her. Fu Hao went on to lead the national army to defeat the Tufang in the north, and more than 20 other small countries such as Yiguo, Bafang, Guifang in the south. In a battle against the Qiangfang forces, Wuding handed over more than half of the dynasty's forces, about 13,000 soldiers, to her command. Fu Hao did not disappoint Wuding. After a fierce battle against the Qiangfang forces, Fu Hao achieved a decisive victory. Through this victory, Fu Hao solved years of warfare, ended harassment on the northwestern border of the Shang Dynasty and made the enemy surrender. Historians believe that this battle that Fu Hao commanded was no less significant than the legendary battle between the Yellow Emperor and Chiyou. It has great significance for the history of China and the Shang Dynasty.

In 1976, archaeologists discovered Fu Hao's mausoleum in the north of Xiaotun village in the western suburbs of Anyang. The tomb is a rectangular pit with a rectangular hole. The tomb is 5.6 meters long from north to south, 4 meters wide from east to west and 8 meters deep. A total of 1928 buried articles, including bronze, jade articles, bone teeth and more than 6,800 pieces of shellfish are placed in the tomb. Among them, Fu Hao steamer (yan) with three bowls, Fu Hao paired vessel (fangyi), Fu Hao owl-shaped vessel (zun), are all rare bronze treasures. The other two copper statues of Fu Hao are the symbol of military power of Fu Hao. Both the inscriptions on the oracle bones and archaeological excavations indicate that the person in the tomb had been a brave female general.

## II. Oracles in Yin Ruins: Symbol of Civilization

A writing system is an important symbol of human civilization. Before the

墓圹为长方形土坑竖穴，南北长 5.6 米，东西宽 4 米，深 8 米。墓内放置随葬品 1 928 件，包括青铜器、玉器、骨牙器等，还有贝币 6 800 余枚。其中，妇好三联甗、妇好偶方彝、妇好鸮尊等均为罕见的青铜器珍品。另外还有两件妇好大铜钺，是死者生前拥有军权的象征。甲骨卜辞和考古发掘都说明墓主生前曾是一员勇猛的女将军。

## 第二节　殷墟甲骨，隶定文明

文字是人类文明的重要标志。甲骨文没有被发现之前，中国有确切纪年的历史只有不到 3 000 年。19 世纪末 20 世纪初，殷墟甲骨文的发现使华夏文明的历史上溯了近千年。

说起甲骨文的发现，还有一段神奇的故事。在清朝光绪年间，一位名叫王懿荣的金石学家，当时是最高学府国子监祭酒（相当于校长）。有一次，他在药店看到一味叫龙骨的中药，上面竟隐隐约约刻着字迹，觉得非常奇怪。他翻看着药渣，没想到居然有一种类似文字的图案，于是他把所有的龙骨都买了下来。经过仔细查验，他发现每片龙骨上都有相似的图案。他把这些奇怪的图案画下来，经过长时间的研究，他确信这是一种文字，而且比较成熟，应该是殷商时期的。后来，人们找到了龙骨出土的地方——河南安阳小屯村，在那里又出土了一大批龙骨。因为这些龙骨主要是龟兽类的甲骨，所以人们将之称为“甲骨文”。

甲骨文被发现之后，引起了学术界的轰动，涌现出了许多著名的古文字学家，如罗振玉（号雪堂）、王国维（号观堂）、董作宾（字彦堂）、郭沫若（字鼎堂）并称为“甲骨四堂”，被誉为甲骨学研究的一代宗师。

甲骨文是商代统治者为了卜问吉凶而留下来的记录，上自国家大事，下至私人生活，如祭祀、征伐、病患、气候、田猎、收成、出门、生育等社会生活的各个方面，是了解商代社会生活的可靠材料。

从 1899 年甲骨文被发现至今，仅从安阳一地就出土了有字的甲骨

oracle bone inscriptions were discovered, China only had a history of less than three thousand years. In the late 19th and early 20th century, the discovery of oracle bone inscriptions in Yin Ruins extended the history of Chinese civilization for nearly a thousand years.

There is a miraculous story about the discovery of the oracle bone inscriptions. During the reign of Emperor Guangxu of the Qing Dynasty, a specialist in epigraphy named Wang Yirong was a member of the highest imperial college of China (equivalent to the President) at that time. He saw a Chinese medicine called Dragon Bone in the pharmacy. It was faintly engraved with characters. He felt very strange. He looked at the residue and found unexpectedly a pattern that looked like words on it, so he bought all the Dragon Bones. After careful inspection, he found a similar pattern on each bone. He drew down these strange patterns. After a long period of research, he was convinced that it was a kind of writing. The characters were developed by the Shang Dynasty. Later, people found the place where the Dragon Bone was unearthed—Xiaotun Village in today's Anyang, Henan Province, where a large number of Dragon Bones were unearthed. These Dragon Bones are called oracle bones because they are mainly bones of turtles and beasts.

The oracle bone inscriptions caused a sensation in the academic world after it was discovered. Many famous specialists in ancient characters emerged. Among them, Luo Zhenyu , Wang Guowei, Dong Zuobin, Guo Moruo were together called the "Four Masters of Oracle Bone" and were known as Grand Masters of oracle bone research.

The oracle bone inscriptions are the records left by the rulers of the Shang Dynasty for predicting good and bad fortunes. It is a reliable material for understanding the social life of the Shang Dynasty, from national events to private life, such as sacrifice, expedition, sickness, climate, field hunting, harvest, visits, birth and other aspects of social life.

Since the discovery of oracle bone inscriptions in 1899, about 150,000 pieces of inscribed bones have been unearthed from Anyang alone. Among them, more than 100 characters at most were inscribed in a single inscription. Scholars have identified more than 4,500 different characters from oracle bone inscriptions, among which about 1,500 characters have been identified. It can be seen that oracle bone inscriptions were already a relatively mature writing system at that time.

约 15 万片，其中单篇卜辞最多者达百余字。学者们已经从甲骨文中分辨出 4500 多个不同的文字图形，其中已经识别的有 1500 多字，可见甲骨文已经是当时比较成熟的文字系统。从掌握的单字情况看，甲骨文已经具备了汉字的象形、会意、形声、指事、转注、假借等 6 种造字方法。

甲骨文的发展经历了 5 个时期，即雄伟期、谨饬期、颓靡期、劲峭期、严整期，时间从盘庚迁殷至武王灭纣，持续了 270 多年。在这段时间里，甲骨文得到飞速发展，并逐渐形成了自己的书写体例。从字体的数量和结构方式上看，甲骨文已经发展成为较严密、系统的文字，汉字的“六书”原则在甲骨文中已有体现。但甲骨文主要特点为：象形字居多，大部分按照物的真实形状或主要特征进行构字；异体字较多，一个字可有十几种甚至几十种写法，字的形体往往以物的形体为标准，有的字笔画较多，有的字笔画较少，大小标准不一；因为字是用刀刻在较硬的甲骨上的，所以笔画较细，方笔居多。以上只是其主要特点，在涉及

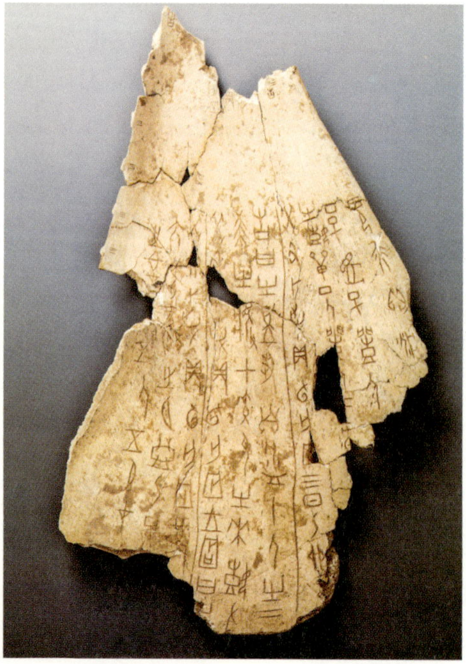

甲骨文

Oracle Bone Inscriptions

Judging from the characters which have been identified, scholars found that oracle bone inscriptions could be identified with six categories of Chinese lexicography: pictographs, compound ideograph, phono-semantic compound, ideograph, derivative cognate and phonetic loan ideogram.

The oracle bone inscriptions had gone through five periods including the majestic period, the cautious period, the decadent season, the stiff period and the strict period. It lasted more than 270 years from King Pangeng to King Wu. During this period, oracle bone inscriptions developed rapidly and gradually formed their own writing style. From the perspective of the number and structure of fonts, Oracle has developed into a more rigorous system of characters. The six categories of Chinese lexicography have been embodied in oracle bone inscriptions. Their main characteristic is the pictographic characters in the majority. Most of them are constructed according to the real shape or the main features. There are many variant characters. Some of which can be written in a dozen or even dozens of ways. A character is usually based on the shape of the object. Some have more strokes and others have less strokes. The criteria are different. Because the word is carved with a knife on the harder bone, so the stroke is smaller. The above are only the main features, and there are many subtle features when it comes to specific words. In a word, oracle bone inscriptions represent the civilization of a specific era, the beginning of Chinese characters and the key to the opening of the great Chinese civilization.

The discovery of the oracle bone inscriptions is of great significance to the study of ancient Chinese civilization. In the oracle bones he collected, the famous scholar Luo Zhenyu discovered the names of kings of the Shang Dynasty. He first proved that Xiaotun village in Anyang now was Yin Ruins in the past. On the basis of Mr. Luo's confirmation, Mr. Wang Guowei confirmed that the King of the Shang Dynasty, Pangeng moved the capital city from Yan (near Qufu in Shandong Province now) to Yin (near Xiaotun village in Anyang now) in 1318 BC. Since then, the capital city was built here and lasted 273 years through 8 generations of 12 kings. These research results have laid a theoretical foundation for the discovery of the oracle bone inscriptions in Yin Ruins. From 1928 AD to 1937 AD, under the leadership of famous archaeologists Dong Zuobin, Li Ji, Liang Siyong, the archaeological group of the Institute of History and Languages of the Academia Sinica carried out archaeological excavations for 10 years and 15 times in Xiaotun

具体的字的时候还有很多细微的特点。总之，甲骨文代表了一个时代的文明，是中国汉字的开端，是开启伟大中华文明的文字钥匙。

甲骨文的发现对研究中国古代文明意义重大。著名学者罗振玉先生在他搜集的甲骨中，发现了刀刻的商王朝先公、先王的名字，首先证明了安阳小屯为殷墟所在地。王国维先生在其基础上，证实了殷墟是盘庚于公元前1318年把都城从奄（今山东曲阜附近）迁到殷（安阳小屯村一带）的，从此历经8代12王，在此建都达273年之久。这些研究成果，为殷墟甲骨文的发掘奠定了理论基础。1928年到1937年间，中央研究院历史语言研究所考古组在著名考古学家董作宾、李济、梁思永等人的带领下，在小屯村一带进行了长达10年共15次的考古发掘，不仅出土了大量的甲骨及玉器、铜器、陶器，而且发现了商代后期的宫殿、宗庙遗址和王陵区，从而正式确立了殷墟为商代王都的证据。殷墟从此成为世界闻名的古文化遗址，影响了中外学术界。

目前，甲骨文已经被认定是中国发现最早、最成体系的文字，甲骨学也已经成为一门蔚为壮观的世界性学科。

## 第三节　安阳殷墟，列遗产名录

经过考证，证实了安阳就是殷墟的所在地。自20世纪初以来，考古人员在安阳境内陆续发现宫殿、王陵和城址等众多遗迹，还有大量的生产工具、生活用具、礼器、乐器和甲骨等遗物，发掘总面积超过24万平方千米。

宫殿宗庙遗址位于河南省安阳市洹河南岸的小屯村、花园庄一带，南北长1 000米，东西宽650米，总面积0.715平方千米，是商王处理政务和居住的场所，也是殷墟最重要的遗址和组成部分，包括宫殿、宗庙等建筑基址80余座。在宫殿宗庙遗址的西、南两面，有一条人工挖掘而成的防御壕沟，将宫殿宗庙环抱其中，起到类似宫城的作用。宫

Village. They not only unearthed a large number of oracle bones, jade wares, bronzes and pottery, but also discovered the palaces, ancestral temple sites and tomb districts of the late Shang Dynasty. Thus it officially proved that the capital of the Shang Dynasty was in Yin Ruins. From then on Yin Ruins has become a world-famous ancient cultural site and affected the entire Chinese and foreign academic circles.

At present, the oracle bone inscriptions have been identified as the earliest and most systematic writing in China. The Oracle Inscription research has also become a spectacular worldwide discipline.

## III. Culture Heritage: Yin Ruins

After research, it was confirmed that Anyang is the location of Yin Ruins. Since the excavation in the early 20th century, archaeologists have discovered many relics of palaces, tombs and city sites in Anyang, as well as a large number of relics of production tools, living utensils, ritual instruments, musical instruments and oracle bones. The total area of exploration has exceeded 240,000 square kilometers.

The site of the palaces and ancestral temples is located in Xiaotun Village and Garden Village on the south bank of Huanhe River in Anyang, Henan Province. It is 1,000 meters long from north to south, 650 meters wide from east to west, and has a total area of 0.715 square kilometers. It is the place where the kings of the Shang Dynasty lived and dealt with national affairs and is also the most important part of Yin Ruins. It includes more than 80 palaces, temples and other building bases. On the west and south sides of this site, there is an artificial defensive trench, which surrounds the palaces and ancestral temples and functions like a city moat. The Tomb District also has the tomb of King Wuding's wife Fu Hao. This is the only tomb which was found to belong to the member of the Shang Dynasty royal family so far and preserved completely. It is also the only royal tomb that is connected with the oracle bone inscriptions and it identifies who was buried, his social status and when he was buried. There are 16 people buried alive in the tomb, and 1,928 pieces of objects, including 468 bronzes, 755 jade articles and 564 pieces of bones and nearly 7,000 sea shells.

The site of royal tomb is located in North Heights of Houjia Village and Wuguan Village on the north bank of Huanhe River in Anyang, Henan Province. It

殿宗庙区还有商代王武丁的配偶妇好的陵墓，这是迄今为止发现的唯一一座保存完整的商王室成员墓葬，也是唯一能与甲骨文联系并断定年代、墓主人及其身份的商代王室成员墓葬。墓室有人殉 16 人，出土器物 1 928 件，包括 468 件青铜器、755 件玉器以及 564 件骨器，另有将近 7 000 枚海贝。

王陵遗址位于河南省安阳市洹河北岸侯家庄与武官村北高地，东西长约 450 米，南北宽约 250 米，总面积约 11 万平方米。自 1934 年以来，在这里累计发现大墓 13 座，陪葬墓、祭祀坑与车马坑 2 000 余处，并出土了数量众多、制作精美的青铜器、玉器、石器、陶器等，是学术界公认的殷商王陵所在地。其中，东区祭祀坑数量众多，排列有序，坑内有不少人、畜骨架，是殷王室祭祀先祖的一个公共祭祀场地，现辟为 M260 展厅。

洹北商城位于河南省安阳市洹河北岸花园庄，城址大体呈方形，东西宽 2.15 千米，南北长 2.2 千米，总面积约 4.7 平方千米，四周有夯筑的城墙基槽。洹北商城遗址的发现，延长了殷商的历史时间，延伸了殷墟的范围。洹北商城遗址的年代早于传统意义上的殷墟晚商文化，略晚于郑州早商文化，很可能是商代中后期的一处都邑遗址。

上述遗址的发现表明，安阳殷墟曾经长期作为商代的都城，具有举足轻重的地位。除此之外，安阳殷墟还出土了目前中国最早最大的青铜器——后母戊鼎。关于后母戊鼎，背后有许多惊心动魄的故事。

1939 年，河南安阳武官村一位叫吴希增的人在野地探宝，在地下 13 米的地方，探杆碰到了一个坚硬的东西，挖出来一看，上面带着铜锈。当晚，他找了十几个人，趁着夜幕动工挖掘，为了不被日本人发现，到天亮再用原土封住洞口。第二天晚上，挖掘队伍扩大到 40 多人，连续挖掘了 3 个晚上，终于抬上来一个铜锈斑斑的庞然大物，这就是震惊后世的国宝后母戊鼎。为了防止日本人抢夺，吴希增的堂弟吴培文想尽了各种办法，他们找到了北平的大古董商肖寅卿，打算卖掉。肖寅卿要求

is about 450 meters long from east to west and 250 meters wide from north to south, with a total area of about 110,000 square meters. Since 1934 AD, 13 large tombs have been discovered here, including more than 2,000 subordinate burial tombs, ritual pits and chariot pits, and a large number of crafted bronzes, jade, stoneware, pottery, which is recognized as the location of the royal tombs of the Shang Dynasty by academic circle. Among them, ritual pits in the Eastern District is numerous and arranged in an orderly manner. There are many human and animal skeletons in the pits. It is a public ritual place for the ancestors of the Yin royal family. It is now the M260 exhibition hall.

The Shang City of Huanbei is located in Garden Village on the north bank of Huanhe River in Anyang, Henan Province. The city site is generally square, 2.15 kilometers wide from east to west, 2.2 kilometers long from north to south, with a total area of about 4.7 square kilometers. The city is surrounded by walled bases. The discovery of the site of the Shang City of Huanbei has extended the history of the Shang Dynasty and extended the scope of Yin Ruins. The Shang City of Huanbei was earlier than the late Shang culture of Yin Ruins, slightly later than the early Shang culture of Zhengzhou, and was probably a city site of the middle and late Shang Dynasty.

The discovery of the above sites shows that Yin Ruins in Anyang has long been the capital of the Shang Dynasty and plays a decisive role. In addition to this, the earliest largest bronze ware at present in China—Houmuwu Ding (bronze square cauldron)—was unearthed from Yin Ruins in Anyang. There are many thrilling stories about Houmuwu Ding.

In 1939 AD, a man named Wu Xizeng from Wuguan Village in Anyang, Henan Province, explored treasure in the wild. At 13 meters underground, he probed a hard object. When the hard object was dug out, it was covered with patina. That night, he got more than 10 people to dig. In order to prevent the Japanese from discovering, they sealed the mouth of the cave with original soil at dawn. The next night, the excavation team expanded to more than 40 people, and continued to excavate for three nights. Finally, a large rusty bronze was dug out. This is the world-shaking Houmuwu Ding, a national treasure. Wu Xizeng's cousin Wu Peiwen tried every means to prevent the Japanese from stealing this treasure. They contacted with Xiao Yinqing, an antique dealer in Peiping, and planned to sell it. Xiao Yinqing

把大鼎分割成几大块装箱，村民们觉得这样是对文物的破坏，于是决心把大鼎好好保护起来。日本人连续派兵进村搜索。第一次，日军 100 多人将吴家大院翻了个底朝天，由于此时大鼎被村民重新埋入地下，日本人无功而返。日本人走后，吴培文将大鼎转移到了自家马棚地下。第二次，日军来了 3 辆大卡车，一进村就架起了机关枪。吴培文急急忙忙检查了马棚的伪装，又泼了些泔水，成功混出了日军包围圈，一直在村外待到天色擦黑。吴培文听到了日本人收兵的哨声，他立刻跑回家，直奔西屋马棚。谢天谢地，大鼎仍在，吴培文大叹"大炉有灵，天助我也"。这之后，吴培文花 20 块大洋从古玩商处买了一个青铜器赝品，藏在自己家炕洞里。不久以后，日本兵和伪军又进村了，直扑吴家后院，扒开吴培文的睡炕，抢走了那个赝品青铜器。但由于日本人仍旧紧盯着吴培文的行踪，要继续搜捕他，为了保护大鼎安全，吴培文将大鼎秘密托付给自家兄弟，远离家乡避难，直到抗战胜利才回到安阳。吴培文等乡亲为保护国宝，在吴家大院 3 次转移埋藏地，最终将其埋藏在吴家大院东屋，免遭日寇掠夺，直至抗战胜利。

1946 年 6 月，当时的安阳政府的一位陈参议打探到大鼎的下落，他劝说吴培文等人把大鼎上交政府。时任安阳县古物保存委员会主任陈子明和国民政府安阳县县长姚法圃带着一班警察，将大鼎从吴家大院东屋挖了出来。曾任国立中央研究院院长的蔡元培先生倡议创建的国立中央博物院（今南京博物院）通过收购、拨交、发掘，集中全国第一流珍品约二三十万件，其中便包括后母戊鼎。1948 年，大鼎在南京首次展出，据记载，蒋介石曾亲临参观，大鼎轰动了整个南京城。1949 年，国民党撤往台湾时有意将大鼎运往台湾，但由于大鼎过于沉重，被遗落在南京飞机场，后被解放军发现，转移到南京博物院。1959 年，北京历史博物馆（今中国国家博物馆）建成，后母戊鼎从南京运往北京，成为"镇馆之宝"，并一直存于国家博物馆，成为中国的"镇国之宝"。

后母戊鼎因鼎腹内壁上铸有"后母戊"三字而得名，鼎呈长方形，

asked to dismember the Ding and put them into several large boxes. The villagers felt that this was a destruction of cultural relics, so they decided to protect the Ding. The Japanese continuously sent troops to the village to search. For the first time, more than 100 Japanese soldiers turned Wu's courtyard upside down. Because the Ding was buried in the ground again by villagers, the Japanese finally came back to nothing. After the Japanese left, Wu Peiwen moved the Ding to the ground beneath his horse shed. The second time, the Japanese army came with three large trucks. When they entered the village, they set up machine guns. Wu Peiwen hurriedly checked the camouflage of the horse shed and poured some swill. Then he successfully went out of the Japanese encirclement. Wu Peiwen had been waiting outside the village till nightfall. After hearing the whistle of Japanese withdrawing troops, he immediately ran home and went straight to the horse shed. Fortunately, the Ding was still there. Wu Peiwen sighed, "The Ding blesses me". After that, Wu Peiwen bought a counterfeit of the Ding from an antique dealer and hid it in the cave under his big bed. Soon after, the Japanese soldiers entered the village again and went straight to the backyard of Wu's courtyard. They found the cave under the bed and took away the fake Ding. However, the Japanese still kept an eye on Wu Peiwen's whereabouts, and they continued to hunt him. In order to protect the Ding, Wu Peiwen entrusted the Ding secretly to his brother and took refuge from his hometown. He didn't return to Anyang until the end of the Anti-Japanese War. In order to protect the national treasure, Wu Peiwen and other folks had changed the buried places of the Ding three times and finally buried it in the east house of Wu's courtyard to avoid being plundered by the Japanese invaders.

In June 1946, a counselor of Anyang government inquired the whereabouts of the Ding. He persuaded Wu Peiwen and others to hand over the Ding to the government. At that time, Chen Ziming, director of Antiquities Preservation Committee in Anyang County, and Yao Fapu, the head of Anyang County Government, took a group of police officers to dig out the Ding from the east house of Wu's courtyard. Mr. Cai Yuanpei, who had been the President of the National Central Research Institute, proposed to build the national central museum (now the Nanjing Museum), which had collected about 200,000 pieces of the country's first-class treasures through acquisition, assignment and excavation, including Houmuwu Ding. In 1948 AD, the Ding was exhibited for the first time in the capital, Nanjing. According to records, Chiang Kai-shek had visited the exhibition in person, and the

口长 112 厘米，口宽 79.2 厘米，壁厚 6 厘米，连耳高 133 厘米，重达 875 千克。鼎身雷纹为地，四周浮雕刻出盘龙及饕餮纹样，反映了中国青铜铸造的超高工艺和艺术水平。“后母戊”是商王武丁的后妃妇好的庙号。在商后期铸造后母戊鼎至少需要 1 000 千克以上的原料，且要在大约二三百名工匠的密切配合下才能完成。经测定，鼎含铜 84.77%、锡 11.64%、铅 2.79%，与古文献记载制鼎的铜锡比例基本相符。

后母戊鼎是迄今为止世界上出土的最大、最重的青铜礼器，享有“镇国之宝”的美誉，现为国家一级文物，2002 年列入禁止出国（境）展览文物名单。

安阳殷墟遗址具有极为重要的文化价值和考古价值：其一，甲骨文的发现和殷墟的发掘证实了中国商王朝的存在，重新构建了中国古代早期历史的框架，使传统文献记载的商代历史成为信史；其二，以宫殿宗庙建筑和王陵大墓为代表的商代建筑，树立了中国古代早期宫殿建筑和皇家墓葬的典范；其三，以青铜器、玉器为代表的殷墟文物证明商朝的青铜冶炼技术非常发达，著名的后母戊鼎重达 875 千克，就是其中的杰

后母戊鼎
The Houmuwu Ding

Ding caused a sensation throughout Nanjing. When the Kuomintang retreated to Taiwan in 1949, they originally planned to transport the Ding to Taiwan. However, because it was too heavy, it was left at the Nanjing Airport and later discovered by the People's Liberation Army and transferred to the Nanjing Museum. In 1959, the Beijing History Museum (now the National Museum of China) was built, and Houmuwu Ding was transferred from Nanjing to Beijing, and became the most precious treasure of the museum and has been kept in the National Museum. It has become the priceless treasure of China.

Houmuwu Ding was named after the "Hou mu wu" inscribed on the inside of the body. The Ding was rectangular, with a mouth length of 112 centimeters, a mouth width of 79.2 centimeters, a wall thickness of 6 centimeters, a connecting ear height of 133 centimeters and a weight of 875 kilograms. The pattern of the Ding body is the ground. Around the relief carved floating dragons and sinister monsters patterns, which reflects the super high craftsmanship and artistic level of Chinese bronze casting. "Houmuwu" is the title of Fu Hao after her death, the wife of King Wuding. The Houmuwu Ding was made in the late Shang Dynasty with at least 1000 kilograms of raw materials and close cooperation of about two or three hundred craftsmen. It is tested that the Ding contains 84.77% of copper, 11.64% of tin and 2.79% of lead, which are basically consistent with the proportion of copper to tin recorded in the ancient documents.

The Houmuwu Ding is the largest and heaviest bronze vessel unearthed in the world until now, and enjoys the reputation of "the priceless treasure of China". It is now a national-level cultural relic. In 2002 AD, it was included in the list of cultural relics forbidden from going abroad.

The Yin Ruins possess extremely important cultural and archaeological values. First, the discovery of the oracle bone inscriptions and the excavation of Yin Ruins confirmed the existence of the Shang Dynasty, reconstructed the framework of the early history of ancient China, and made the history of Shang Dynasty recorded in the traditional literature a true history. Secondly, architecture of the Shang Dynasty, represented by the palace, ancestral temple and royal tomb, has established a model of ancient Chinese palace architecture and royal tombs. Thirdly, Yin Ruins' cultural relics represented by bronzes and jade articles have proved that the bronze smelting technology of the Shang Dynasty was very developed. The famous Houmuwu Ding,

出代表，为商代文明提供了重要的证据；其四，从 1928 年开始的殷墟考古发掘至今，培养了一批批的考古学者，殷墟成为中国考古学的摇篮；其五，多达 15 万片的甲骨，吸引了众多的学者投身于其中，创立了一门新的学问——甲骨学。有鉴于其重大的历史和文物价值，2007 年，安阳殷墟被联合国教科文组织列入《世界遗产名录》。

## 第四节　曹魏建邺，再为乱世都城

商朝灭亡后的 1 000 多年间，没有王朝在安阳建都，直到公元 204 年，曹操攻占了邺城（今河北临漳县西及河南安阳市北郊），在袁绍经营的基础上，才对其进行了重新规划与设计，营建改造，使邺城成为当时首屈一指的政治、军事、经济和文化中心。曹操虽然当时已具有了“挟天子以令诸侯”的能力，但他并未称帝，当时的首都在许（今许昌市），邺城仍为大汉统辖之下的一个城邑。

为什么曹操会选择邺城作为自己的王都呢？大致有以下几个方面的原因：一是邺城有山河之固，西依巍巍太行，南望滔滔黄河，在军事上可谓山河险固，可进可退，可攻可守；二是交通便利，邺城南北为广袤的大平原，自古为南北通衢，自西向东，有漳、滏、洹诸水穿过，舟楫便利；三是邺地富庶，土地肥沃，适宜农业耕作，物产丰富；四是有利于军事和政治的发展，军事上来看，整个北方已经平定，南有孙权、刘表相接，西有马超、韩遂虎视，加之枭雄刘备，临近这些地区建都是极不安全的。从政治上来看，曹操为汉丞相，与汉献帝为君臣关系，其府邸远离许都，可以避免许多早请示晚汇报的麻烦，也避免别人说他“挟天子以令诸侯”。不但如此，他还把邺城作为自己的安葬之处。据《三国志》记载，公元 220 年，曹操卒于洛阳，灵柩运到了邺城。2009 年，考古工作者在安阳市安丰乡西高穴村南发现了曹操的高陵墓。

据文献记载，曹操在邺城进行了一系列的建设活动。公元 208 年

which weighs 875 kilograms, is an outstanding representative and provides important evidence for the tradition and civilization of the Shang Dynasty. Fourthly, since the archaeological excavation of Yin Ruins in 1928 AD, a number of archaeologists have been trained, and Yin Ruins have become the cradle of Chinese archaeology. Fifthly, as many as 150,000 pieces of oracle bones attracted many scholars to join in and a new discipline of Oracle Bone has been created. In view of its significant values of historical and cultural heritage, Yin Ruins in Anyang was listed on *The World Heritage List* by UNESCO in 2007 AD.

## IV. Yecheng: A Capital in Troubled Times

In the more than 1,000 years after the demise of the Shang Dynasty, no dynasties built their capitals here. Until 204 AD, Cao Cao had conquered Yecheng (now the west of Linzhang County, Hebei Province, and the northern suburb of Anyang City, Henan Province) and re-established it on the basis of Yuan Shao's management. Planning and design, construction and transformation made Yecheng the political, military, economic and cultural center that was second to none. Although Cao Cao had the power to "control the emperor to command the nobles" at the time, he did not claim to be the emperor. At that time, the capital was Xu (now Xuchang City), and Yecheng was still a city under the jurisdiction of the Han Dynasty.

Why did Cao Cao choose Yecheng as his own fief? There were roughly the following reasons. First, there were mountains and rivers in Yecheng. Yecheng was situated to Taihang Mountain in the west, and the Yellow River was in the south. In terms of military, it could be said that the mountains and rivers in Yecheng were strongly defendable, and it was easy to make attack-defend and advance-retreat strategies. Secondly, the transportation was convenient. To the north and south sides of the city were the vast plains. Since ancient times, they had been the north-south thoroughfare. From the west to the east, Zhanghe River, Fuhe River and Huanhe River flow through, and water transport was very convenient. Thirdly, Yecheng was rich. Fertile land was suitable for agricultural farming, and products were abundant. Fourthly, it is conducive to military and political development. From a military perspective, the whole north had been settled, but with Sun Quan (182 AD–252

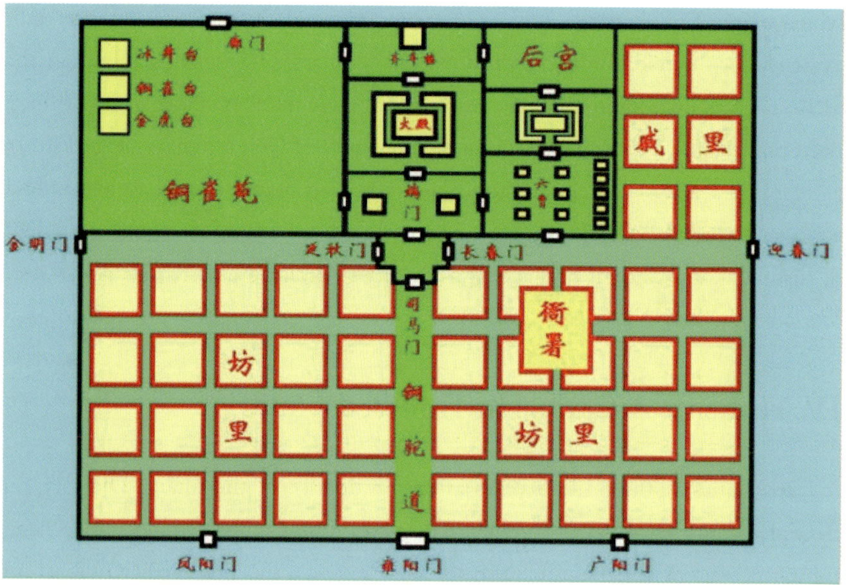


曹魏邺城复原图

The restoration map of Yecheng in the state of Wei ruled by Cao Cao

在邺城修建了玄武池。这是一个巨大的人工湖泊，位于邺城铜雀台南8 000米处，赤壁之战中曹操的水军就是在这里展开训练的。公元210年，建造铜雀台。曹操消灭袁氏兄弟后，夜宿邺城，半夜之时见到金光从地面升起，第二天从地下挖到一只铜雀。大臣荀攸说，从前舜的母亲梦见玉雀进入怀中而生下了舜，现在曹操得到了铜雀也是吉祥的征兆。曹操非常高兴，于是就在漳水之上建造了铜雀台来表彰自己平定天下的功绩。铜雀台高约33米，上面有100多间房屋。公元213年，曹操在邺城修建了金虎台。金虎台位于邺城的西北部，在铜雀台的南边，高约27米，台上有135间房屋。公元214年，曹操在邺城修建了冰井台。冰井台位于铜雀台的北边，因为上面有冰井而得名，高约27米，有140间房屋。冰井台上有3个冰室，每个冰室内有多个冰井，井深约50米，储藏着大量的冰块、煤炭、粮食和食盐，具有战备意义。

考古工作者认为曹魏邺城具有三个特征：一是规模宏大，城墙东西

AD) and Liu Biao (142 AD–208 AD) in the south, Ma Chao (176 AD–222 AD) and Han Sui (?–215 AD) in the west as well as ambitious Liu Bei (161 AD–223 AD). It was insecure to build the capital near these places. From the perspective of politics, Cao Cao was the Prime Minister of the Han Dynasty and was inferior to Emperor Xian of the Han Dynasty. His residence was far from the capital Xu. So he avoided the trouble of asking Emperor Xian for instructions, and also avoided the trouble of others saying that he "control the emperor to command the nobles". Not only that, but he also made Yecheng his burial place. According to the *Records of the Three Kingdoms*: in 220 AD, Cao Cao died in Luoyang, and his coffin was transported to Yecheng. In 2009, archaeologists discovered Cao Cao's tomb in the south of Xigaoxue Village in Anfeng County of Anyang City.

According to the records, Cao Cao carried out a series of construction activities in Yecheng. In 208 AD, Xuanwu Pool was built in Yecheng. This was a huge artificial lake, 8,000 meters to the south of Bronze Sparrow Terrace in Yecheng, where Cao's water troops were trained for the battle of Chibi. In 210 AD, Bronze Sparrow Terrace was built. After Cao Cao killed the Yuan brothers (Yuan Shao's sons: Yuan Shang and Yuan Xi), he stayed overnight in Yecheng. In the middle of the night, he saw gold lights rising from the ground. The next day, a copper sparrow was dug out of the ground. The minister Xun You said that King Shun's mother had dreamed that a jade sparrow came into her arms and later she gave birth to Shun. So now getting the copper sparrow was also a good sign. Cao Cao was very glad, so he built Bronze Sparrow Terrace over Zhangshui River to celebrate his achievement of pacifying the states. Bronze Sparrow Terrace was 33 meters high and had more than 100 rooms. In 213 AD, Cao Cao built Gold Tiger Terrace in Yecheng. Gold Tiger Terrace was located in the northwest of Yecheng, on the south side of Bronze Sparrow Terrace. It was 27 meters high, and had 135 rooms. In 214 AD, Cao Cao built Ice Well Terrace in Yecheng. Ice Well Terrace was located on the north side of Bronze Sparrow Terrace. It was named after an ice well on it. It was 27 meters high and had 140 rooms. There were three ice chambers on the Ice Well Terrace. And there were several ice wells in each ice chamber. The well was 50 meters deep and stored a large amount of ice, coal, grain and salt. It was of strategic importance.

Archaeologists believe that Yecheng in State of Wei ruled by Cao Cao has three following characteristics. First, the scale was huge. The city wall was 3.5 kilometers

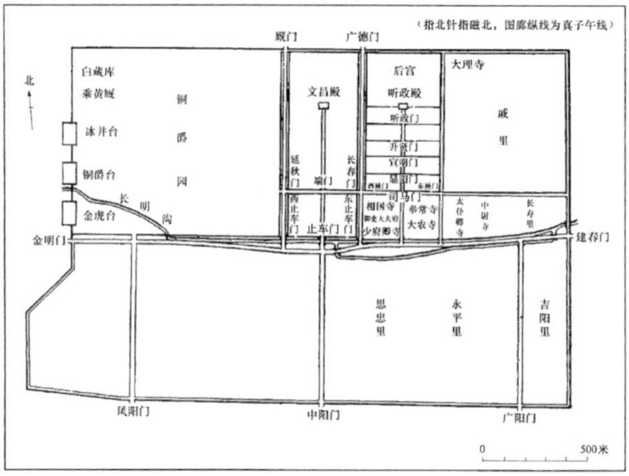

涿州影视城复原的邺城铜雀台
Restored Bronze Sparrow Terrace by Zhuozhou Film and Television City

长 3.5 千米，南北 2.5 千米，四面共有 7 个城门，分别是南面的凤阳门、中阳门、广阳门，东面的建春门，北面的广德门、厩门，西面的金明门；二是布局严整，北部是宫殿政务区，西边是苑囿（即铜雀园，曹魏时称铜爵园），东边为戚里，南部为居民和市场交易区，两区之间由中心街道隔开，帝王宫殿坐落在城北部，这种规制改变了汉代以来宫殿区分散的布局，开创了此后帝都王都城市布局的先河；三是城墙“饰表以砖”，也就是我们后世所见到的中间夯土，然后在外层砌砖的砖城墙，这在城市建筑史上具有开创性的意义。

公元 335 年，后赵石虎迁都于邺，开始了大规模的建造活动，使邺城进入了其发展史上的鼎盛时期。后赵重建邺城经历了前后两个时期：前期为石勒时期，主要是都城设计与邺宫初造；后期为石虎时期，根据石勒总体设计大规模营建，先城内后城外，宫殿建筑先内宫后大朝。以九华宫、太武殿及两侧东西阁为主体工程，宫城、郭城围绕主体工程布置，自北向南，由北城垣上齐斗楼，经太武殿、端门及中阳门内大街、中阳门，构成全城南北中轴线，宫殿建筑、官署、街区、里巷等均沿中轴线左右对称，街区呈棋盘状，全城平面布局大体呈现横长方形，城门

long from east to west, 2.5 kilometers from north to south, and there were 7 gates on all sides. They were Fengyang Gate, Zhongyang Gate and Guangyang Gate in the south, Jianchun Gate in the east, Guangde Gate and Jiu Gate in the north, and Jinming Gate in the west. Secondly, the layout was neat. In the north was the palace administrative district, in the west was the garden (namely the Copper Sparrow Garden), and in the east was the district where Emperor's relatives lived, and in the south was the residential and market trading area. The two districts were separated by a central street. The imperial palace was located in the northern part of the city. This regulation changed the scattered layout of the palace area since the Han Dynasty and created the precedent of the later imperial capital. Thirdly, the city wall was decorated with bricks in the outer layer. It is the rammed earth in the middle that we see later, and the brick walls that were laid in the outer layer, which have a groundbreaking significance in the history of urban architecture.

In 335 AD, Emperor Shi Hu of the Later Zhao Dynasty moved the capital to Yecheng, and began a large-scale construction, which made Yecheng enter its heyday as a capital. The reconstruction of Yecheng in Later Zhao experienced two periods. The previous period was Shi Le period, mainly for the design of the capital city and initial building of the palaces. The later period was Shi Hu period. According to the overall design by Shi Le, large-scale construction was carried out, first inside the city and then outside the city. In terms of the construction of palaces, the inner palaces were built first and then the imperial court. With Jiuhua Palace, Taiwu Hall, East and West Pavilions on both sides were the main projects, palace area and the outer city were arranged around them. The north-south axis of the whole city went from the north city wall to the Qidou Building, through the Taiwu Hall, (the end gate), Zhongyang Gate Street and Zhongyang Gate. The palace buildings, government offices, blocks and lanes were all symmetrical along the central axis. The blocks were in the shape of a checkerboard. The layout of the whole city presented generally horizontal rectangular. East, south, west, north and clockwise, the gates were in order of Jianchun, Guangyang, Zhongyang, Fengyang, Jinming, Jiumen, Guangde. The gates were named after the four seasons. The layout of the city followed the configurations of stars in the sky. City wall, city gate, three towers, palaces, streets and lanes, customs and ceremonial architecture were not only neatly planned, but also had a high artistic level.

Ran Wei had built the capital in Yecheng for 2 years, but it did not carry out

自东、南、西、北顺时针，依次为建春、广阳、中阳、凤阳、金明、厩门、广德等，门名取象“四时”命设，城制设计具有“天象”意识。城垣与城门、三台、宫殿、街市里巷、习俗、礼制建筑等，不仅规划整齐，而且具有较高的艺术水平。

冉魏都邺两年，没有对邺城进行加固和建设。公元 357 年，前燕迁都邺城，修复邺宫和铜雀、金虎、冰井三台。公元 535 年，东魏因为邺城狭小而增筑了南城，把原来的邺城变为北城。北齐在邺建都共 27 年，没有进行大的修缮活动。公元 580 年，邺城被焚毁。

自曹操都邺到北齐灭亡，邺城战火不断，是各种势力争夺的焦点，王室宫殿损毁尤其严重。总的来看，对邺城的建设主要集中在曹魏和后赵两个阶段，之后的几个王朝主要是对铜雀、金虎、冰井三台的整修和加固。乱世之中的邺城，最终化为灰烬。

## 第五节　古都安阳历史名人轶事

安阳历史悠久，人物古迹众多，为后人留下了丰富的文化遗产，在中国古都史上有着独特的历史地位。

### 1. 文王拘而演《周易》

周文王姬昌任西伯侯期间被殷纣王囚禁于羑里（今安阳汤阴）。在被囚禁的 7 年里，他将伏羲的“先天八卦”改造成“后天八卦”，之后又进一步将其推演成六十四卦并系以卦爻辞，完成了《周易》这部千古不朽的著作。这就是所谓的“文王拘而演《周易》”。《周易》可以说是我国文化的源头，它的内容极其丰富，对中国几千年来的政治、经济、文化等各个领域都产生了极其深刻的影响，是我国古代一部关于自然科学和社会科学的经典之作。《周易》以占筮的形式推测自然和社会的变

any reinforcement or construction of Yecheng. In 357 AD, the Former Yan Dynasty moved to Yecheng, and repaired the palace and Bronze Sparrow Terrace, Gold Tiger Terrace and Ice Well Terrace. In 535 AD, the Eastern Wei Dynasty expanded the South City because of the narrowness of Yecheng, and turned the original Yecheng into the North City. The Northern Qi Dynasty had been in Yecheng for 27 years and had not carried out any major repair works. In 580 AD, Yecheng was burned down.

From the construction of Yecheng by Cao Cao to the demise of Northern Qi, the war in Yecheng had continued, and Yecheng was the focus of all kinds of power. Especially the royal palaces were damaged greatly. In general, the construction of Yecheng was mainly made on the times of Cao Cao and Later Zhao, while renovation and reinforcement of Bronze Sparrow Terrace, Gold Tiger Terrace and Ice Well Terrace were carried out in the following dynasties. However, unfortunately, Yecheng was finally burned into ashes later during warfare.

## V. The Famous Historical Figures of Ancient Anyang

Anyang has a long history and numerous historical figures. It has left a rich cultural heritage for future generations and has a unique historical position in the history of ancient capitals of China.

### 1. King Wen deduced *The Book of Changes* (*Zhou Yi*) in Youli

Ji Chang, later known as King Wen of the Zhou Dynasty, was imprisoned in Youli (now Tangyin County, Anyang ) by Emperor Zhou of the Yin Dynasty when he was Marquis of Xibo. In the seven years of his imprisonment, he transformed Fuxi's primordial "ba gua" , which was an ancient fortune telling device. The ancient "ba gua" device had eight directions, exactly like a compass. This ancient "ba gua" device was used to predict the future. Later, he further promoted it into sixty-four trigrams and made a remark, completing the great work of *The Book of Changes*. This was the so-called story of King Wen's deduction of *The Book of Changes* in his imprisonment. *The Book of Changes* can be said to be the source of Chinese culture. Its content is extremely rich, and it has exerted a profound influence on China's political, economic, cultural and other fields for thousands of years. It is a classic about natural science and social science in ancient China. *The Book of Changes* speculates the changes of nature and society in the form of divination. It covers

化，内容几乎涵盖了人类社会的全部内容，被誉为“群经之首”。

### 2. 西门豹投巫治邺地

西门豹，战国时期魏国人，著名的政治家、军事家、水利家，同时也是我国历史上著名的无神论者。魏文侯在位时，西门豹任邺（安阳）令，其治邺的故事传为千古美谈。西门豹上任伊始，发现这里的官员借为河伯“娶妻”之名，每年都要向百姓征收大笔钱财，而真正用于“娶妻”的只是这些钱财中的一小部分，其余的都被这些地方官和巫婆们贪污了。河伯娶媳妇使得那些有漂亮女子的人家担心大巫婆替河伯娶她们，大多带着自己的女儿逃跑了。于是，西门豹命令差役们将大巫婆抛到了河中，让她与河神商量能否更换人选，连续把 3 个巫婆抛到河中后，其余的地方官员都吓得在地上叩头，大声求饶。从此以后，再也没有人敢提为河伯娶媳妇的事了。西门豹带领百姓治理邺地，开挖了 12 条渠道，把黄河水引来灌溉农田，从此邺县恢复了生机，西门豹治邺获得了巨大的成功。

### 3. 项羽破釜沉舟

项羽是秦末反秦武装力量楚国的将领。公元前 208 年，秦将章邯镇压陈胜、吴广起义之后，又攻破邯郸，赵王歇及张耳率领的反秦武装被迫退守巨鹿（今河北平乡西南），被秦将王离率 20 万人围困。项羽率领军队渡黄河前去营救赵国，以解巨鹿之围。待楚军全部渡过漳河以后，项羽让士兵们饱饱地吃了一顿饭，每人再带 3 天的干粮，然后传下命令：把渡河的船（古代称舟）凿穿沉入河底，把做饭用的锅（古代称釜）砸个粉碎，把附近的房屋放把火统统烧毁。这就叫“破釜沉舟”。项羽用这办法来表示他有进无退、一定要夺取胜利的决心。就这样，没有退路

almost all the aspects of human society, and is honored as the "Head of the Sutras".

**2. Ximen Bao killed the witches and ruled County Ye**

Ximen Bao was in the State of Wei in the Warring States Period. He was a famous politician, military strategist, hydraulic engineer, and also a famous atheist in Chinese history. Marquis Wen of Wei appointed Ximen Bao as the magistrate of County Ye. The story of his ruling was passed down through the ages. At the beginning of his ruling in Ye, Ximen Bao found that local officials here collected large sums of money from people every year in the name of the river god's marriage. What was really used for marriage was only a small part of the money, and the rest was embezzled by local officials and witches. The event that the witches chose a girl for the river god as his wife every year made those who had beautiful daughters run away because of worries about their own daughters. Therefore, Ximen Bao ordered the servants to throw a witch into the river, letting her discuss with the river god. After three witches were consecutively thrown into the river, the local officials were scared to kneel and beg for mercy. Since then, no one had ever dared to mention the river god's wife. Ximen Bao led the people to develop Ye and excavated 12 channels to draw the Yellow River water to irrigate the farmland. From then on, County Ye had recovered its vitality. Ximen Bao succeeded in ruling County Ye.

**3. Xiang Yu burned the boats**

Xiang Yu was a general from State of Chu during the peasant uprising in the late Qin Dynasty. In 208 BC, after Zhang Han, general of the Qin Dynasty, suppressed the uprising led by Chen Sheng and Wu Guang, and occupied Handan, King Xie of the State of Zhao and Zhang Er, who were against the Qin army, were forced to retreat to Julu (now southwest of Pingxiang, Hebei), and were besieged by Qin army of 200,000 led by General Wang Li. Xiang Yu led the Chu army across the Yellow River to rescue the State of Zhao, which was his ally. Xiang Yu went to Julu to rescue the Zhao army, which was under siege. After all the Chu soldiers had crossed Zhanghe River, Xiang Yu let them have a full meal, then each with three days of rations, and gave the order: to chisel the boats and sink them into the river, to smash the pots of cooking and to burn down all the houses nearby. The idiom originated from the Battle of Julu was called "breaking cauldrons and sinking boats", which was later used to reveal one's determination to achieve one's goal at any cost. Xiang Yu used this method to indicate that he was determined to win the war. In this way, the soldiers who had no way out were intrepid and fearless. After nine fierce battles, the Chu army eventually defeated the Qin army. Several generals of the Qin army, some

的楚军战士以一当十，杀伐声惊天动地。经过 9 次激战，楚军最终大破秦军。秦军的几个主将，有的被杀，有的当了俘虏，有的投了降。这一仗不但解了巨鹿之围，而且把秦军打得再也振作不起来，两年之后秦朝就灭亡了。

### 4. 欧阳修作赋秋声楼

欧阳文忠公书院是北宋著名政治家、文学家、史学家欧阳修任滑州通判时的住所，是全国四大书院之一，位于安阳滑县古城内东南隅，原名秋声书院，亦称欧阳书院，又名画舫书院。书院内建有富丽堂皇的画舫斋和秋声楼。画舫斋是欧阳修的“燕私之居”，为欧阳修所造。秋声楼位于画舫斋之后，因《秋声赋》在这里所作而得名。

### 5. 岳飞精忠报国

岳飞（1103—1142），南宋军事家，民族英雄，相州汤阴（今安阳汤阴）人。岳飞十五六岁时，北方的金人南侵，宋朝当权者腐败无能，节节败退，国家处在生死存亡的关头。

一天，岳母把岳飞叫到跟前，说：“现在国难当头，你有什么打算？”岳飞说：“到前线杀敌，精忠报国！”岳母听了儿子的回答，十分满意。“精忠报国”正是母亲对儿子的期望，她决定把这 4 个字刺在儿子的背上，让他永远记着这一誓言。岳飞解开上衣，请母亲下针。岳母问：“你怕痛吗？”岳飞说：“小小钢针算不了什么，如果连针都怕，怎么去前线打仗！”岳母先在岳飞背上写了字，然后用绣花针刺了起来，刺完之后又涂上醋墨。从此，“精忠报国”4 个字就永不褪色地留在了岳飞的后背上。后来，岳飞以“精忠报国”为座右铭，奔赴前线，英勇杀敌，立下赫赫战功，成为一名抗金名将。

were killed, some became prisoners, and the others surrendered. This battle not only broke the siege in Julu, but also struck the Qin army greatly. Two years later, the Qin Dynasty was destroyed.

**4. Ouyang Xiu wrote poetry in the Qiusheng Pavilion**

Ouyang Wenzhong Academy was the residence of Ouyang Xiu, who was a famous politician, writer and historian in the Northern Song Dynasty, when he was appointed as the judge of Huazhou. It was one of the four great academies in China and was located in the southeast corner of the ancient city of County Hua in Anyang. It was formerly known as Qiusheng Academy. Qiusheng Academy was also known as Ouyang Academy and the Painting Academy. There were the magnificent Huafang Studio and the Qiusheng Pavilion. Huafang Studio was Ouyang Xiu's "Swallow's Private Residence", which was created by him. Qiusheng Pavilion was located behind Huafang Studio, and became famous for the poem *Qiusheng Fu* that was written inside Qiusheng Pavilion.

**5. Patriot: Yue Fei**

Yue Fei, was a strategist and a national hero of the Southern Song Dynasty. He was born in Tangyin, Xiangzhou (now Tangyin in Anyang). When Yue Fei was fifteen or sixteen years old, the Song Dynasty was invaded from the North by the state of Jin. The government and higher authorities of the Song Dynasty were so corrupt and incompetent that the country was at a critical juncture.

One day, Yue Fei's mother said to him, "Now the country is in a difficult time, what are your plans?" Yue Fei said, "Go to the front line, kill the enemy and be loyal to the country!" His mother was very satisfied with his answer, because "serve the country with the utmost loyalty" was her requirement for her son. She decided to tattoo the characters on the back of her son and let him remember this oath forever. When Yue Fei untied his shirt, his mother asked, "Are you afraid of pain?" Yue Fei said, "A small steel needle is nothing. If you are afraid of even the needle, how can you go to the front line to fight?" Yue Fei's mother first wrote four words " jing zhong bao guo" (literary meaning "serve the country with the utmost loyalty") on Yue Fei's back, and then stabbed the characters with an embroidery needle. After that, his mother coated them with vinegar ink. Since then, the four Chinese characters "jing zhong bao guo" were never wiped out from Yue Fei's back. Later, Yue Fei took it as his motto and went to the front line to kill the enemy and became a famous hero fighting against the Jin intruders.

第四章

# 五朝古都——郑州

Chapter Ⅳ

# Zhengzhou: The Ancient Capital City of Five Dynasties

郑州，河南省省会，地处中原腹地、九州之中，北临黄河，西依洛阳，南部与许昌、平顶山接壤，东接开封，是一座有着悠久历史的文化名城。它曾 5 次为都，先后为中华人文始祖黄帝之都、第一个奴隶制王朝夏朝的都城、商朝前期和中期的都城、春秋时期郑国的都城、战国时期韩国的都城，是中国最早的古都和中国早期文明的亲历者。中国目前公认的古都中，郑州和其他古都不太一样，它是中华早期文明的都城，而其他古都大都是中国封建社会时期的都城。中国的政治制度、思想源流、科技成就、文化源头等都在这片古老的大地上孕育、发生，郑州犹如一位饱经沧桑的老人，见证了中华文明早期的辉煌。只是当时光来到现代，这位老人似乎离我们太过遥远，许多人淡忘了他。1993 年，在中国殷商文化学会主持召开的郑州商城与殷商文明国际研讨会上，胡厚宣、邹衡等 32 位国内外知名专家学者联名倡议将郑州列入全国八大古都之一。2003 年，在北京召开的郑州商都 3 600 年学术座谈会上，几十位专家学者又一次联名呼吁把郑州列为中国八大古都之一。2004 年，中国古都学会第 21 届学术研讨会上，来自全国各地的上百位古都学、历史学、考古学专家聚会郑州，再一次对郑州的古都地位、历史演变、保护利用进行了深入研讨，一致赞同古都郑州应列为中国八大古都之一，与北京、西安、洛阳、安阳、开封、南京、杭州并列。

## 第一节　轩辕故里，黄帝之都

轩辕黄帝，是中国人心中的感情基点，是中华民族的人文始祖，每一个中国人几乎都能在轩辕黄帝那里找到自己的心灵的根。中华民族有强大的向心力和坚如磐石的凝聚力就是这个原因，这也是中华民族继往开来的历史根基。祖宗观念是神圣的，同根同祖的中国人都是轩辕黄帝的后裔。黄帝创造了丰富的物质文明，如舟、车等，中国人普遍认为黄帝时代是中华文明萌芽的年代。

Zhengzhou, the provincial capital of Henan Province, is located in the hinterland of Central Plains, connecting Yellow River in the north, Luoyang in the west, Xuchang and Pingdingshan in the south and Kaifeng in the east. As a famous cultural city with a long history, it has ever served as the ancient capital city for five times in Chinese history: the earliest capital city during the time of the Yellow Emperor (the ancestor of the Chinese people); the capital city of the Xia Dynasty (the first slavery dynasty); the capital of the early and mid-Shang Dynasty; the capital of Zheng during the Spring and Autumn Period, and the capital of Han during the Warring States Period. As the earliest ancient capital in Chinese history, Zhengzhou paved the way for early Chinese civilization. Among the great ancient capital cities in China, Zhengzhou is seen as the capital of China's early civilization. Zhengzhou nurtured China's political system, origin of Chinese philosophy, scientific and technological achievements, and cultural origins. Zhengzhou is like an old man who has experienced diversity and witnessed the early glory of Chinese civilization. However, when it comes to modern society, the glories of this city seem to be forgotten. In 1993 AD, The International Symposium on Zhengzhou Shang Civilization was hosted by the China Association of Shang Civilization. 32 domestic and foreign well-known experts including Hu Houyi and Zou Heng proposed that Zhengzhou should be included in the eight ancient capitals of China. In 2003 AD, the academic symposium on the 3600-year-old Zhengzhou Shang Capital was held in Beijing. Dozens of experts and scholars called for Zhengzhou to be listed as one of the ancient capitals of China. At the end of 2004 AD, hundreds of ancient scholars, history and archaeology experts from all over the country gathered in Zhengzhou at the 21st Academic Symposium of the Association of Ancient Chinese Capitals, and once again discussed Zhengzhou's status, historical evolution, protection and utilization. It is unanimously agreed that Zhengzhou should be listed as one of the eight ancient capitals of China, alongside Beijing, Xi'an, Luoyang, Anyang, Kaifeng, Nanjing and Hangzhou.

## I. Yellow Emperor's Birthplace and His Capital

The Yellow Emperor (Huang Di), who is widely recognized as a common ancestor of all Han Chinese, connects all Chinese people around the world. Every

根据历史记载，黄帝时期的都城是有熊。新郑市就是古代的有熊城。黄帝住在这里的一个叫轩辕的丘陵上，所以黄帝也以“轩辕”为名。新石器时代，洪水灾害比比皆是，选择丘陵恰好反映了先民们有意避开洪水而择地居住的智慧。在黄帝之后的2 000多年间，“有熊”这个名称一直沿用。《史记》里曾提到“有熊出良马”，故事是这样的：商朝末年，纣王无道，施政错乱。他听信谗言，将西伯侯姬昌囚禁在羑里这个地方，姬昌手下的谋士闳夭等人非常着急，就想了一个办法来救姬昌。他们根据纣王又贪财又好色这个毛病，就从这两个方面来贿赂纣王。他们想办法从有莘氏那里找来许多美女，从骊戎那里找来极漂亮的马，又从有熊国那里找来36匹良马，再加上其他一些珍宝，统统献给纣王。昏庸的商纣王一高兴，就把姬昌给放了。姬昌回到自己的封国后，励精图治，积攒力量，国势蒸蒸日上。到了周武王姬发时，纣王终于被消灭。

中国人心中的黄帝，不仅是中国先民们一位伟大首领的象征，而且是一个部落联盟的代表。根据历史记载，黄帝时期有10世之多，前后有1 000多年。黄帝活动的区域非常广阔，以郑州为中心，向外辐射到今天的河南、河北、山东、陕西、甘肃、湖南、湖北等地。历史记载，黄帝曾和炎帝大战于阪泉之野。阪泉这个地方，大家争论不一，但无外乎现在的陕西和河南这两个区域；黄帝曾和蚩尤大战于涿鹿，取得大胜，涿鹿这个地方在今天河北的中部；黄帝曾经向东到达大海，沿途封禅了泰山，又向南到达了湘，也就是今天的湖南这个地方；黄帝曾经在荆山下铸鼎，现在河南省灵宝市荆山这个地方还有黄帝铸鼎的遗迹；黄帝曾经登过泰山、太室山、华山、首山、东莱山，他在这些山中得到了上天的感应，这些山大都位于现在的陕西、河南、山东等地。

民间传说也从一个侧面反映了郑州地区曾是黄帝时代先民活动的中心。传说远古时候，黄帝和炎帝摒弃前嫌，讲和联盟，两个部落合并成为炎黄部族，共同开发中原，种田建房，逐渐富足强盛起来。东南方的部落首领蚩尤生性暴戾乖张，他听说中原地带是风水宝地，就大肆向中

Chinese can find the root of their soul in the Xuanyuan Culture. For this reason, we can say that the historical root of Chinese nation comes from Chinese nation's strong unity and rock-solid cohesiveness. The ancestral concept is sacred and the Chinese people regard themselves as the descendants of the Yellow Emperor Xuanyuan. The Yellow Emperor created a rich civilization. Chinese believe that the era of the Yellow Emperor was the beginning of Chinese civilization.

According to historical records, the Yellow Emperor built the capital in the city of Youxiong (modern Xinzheng City). The Yellow Emperor lived on a hill which was called "Xuanyuan". Therefore, the Yellow Emperor also took the name of "Xuanyuan". In the Neolithic Age, floods abounded, and living on hills reflected the wisdom of the ancestors who had known how to avoid natural disaster by choosing a proper living place. The name "Youxiong" was used in the later 2,000 years following the Yellow Emperor. In *Shi Ji* (*Records of the Historian*), it was mentioned that there were a lot of good horses in the city of Youxiong. According to the document, the King Zhou of the Shang Dynasty, was incompetent and the government was in disorder. King Zhou listened to bad advice from his officials and imprisoned Ji Chang, the Marquis of Xibo, in Youli. Ji Chang's counselors and men were very worried and devised a plan to save Ji Chang. Because they knew that King Zhou was greedy and lascivious, they bribed King Zhou in two ways. They tried their best to find a lot of beautiful women from Youshenshi and beautiful horses from Lirong, 36 horses from the Youxiong, and some other treasures. Then they dedicated all of it to King Zhou. The fatuous King Zhou of Shang was so pleased that he let Ji Chang go. After Ji Chang returned to his own province, he made great efforts to make his province rich, and his efforts made the province flourish. Ji Chang went to war against King Zhou and defeated him in battle. After Ji Fa (the son of Ji Chang) was victorious in battle against King Zhou, he became King Wu of Zhou.

The Yellow Emperor was not only a great leader, but also a representative of a tribal alliance in ancient time. According to historical records, during 1,000 years there were as many as 10 generations of descendants in the Yellow Emperor period. The broad regions where the Yellow Emperor had ever lived were centered in Zhengzhou, extending out to today's Henan, Shandong, Shaanxi,Gansu, Hunan, Hubei and other provinces. According to historical records, the Yellow Emperor and Emperor Yan fought in the wilderness of Banquan. Scholars debate whether or not

原侵吞抢掠。黄帝组织炎黄族众在涿鹿迎战蚩尤。当时正是中秋时节，夜寒昼热，时常大雾弥漫，黄帝在作战中往往迷失方向，战事屡屡受挫。为了打败蚩尤，黄帝到处探察访问，终于发现一种磁石可以定位指向。他据此研制成一个木头人，用磁石琢磨成一只手臂，五指始终指向南方，叫它为“方”；研制了一架车，在宽平的木板下装上能转动的圆轮，前头装上扶手，叫“轩”；在“轩”前面安上两根木杠，使“轩”可以推拉走动，叫“辕”。黄帝将这天下第一器械定名为“轩辕方”。黄帝用它来确定方向，终于战胜了蚩尤。这个民间故事，流传于现在的新郑一带。

还有一个仓颉造字的传说也反映了黄帝时期的一些史实。古时候没有文字，人们结绳记事。轩辕黄帝命大臣仓颉造字，仓颉在洧水河南岸的一个高台上造屋住下，专心造字。好长时间也没造出字来，仓颉很着急。一天他正坐在茅屋前苦想，一只凤凰鸣叫着从天空飞过，凤凰嘴里衔的一片树叶落下来，上面有个明显的兽蹄印。一名老猎人说这是貅蹄印，各种兽的蹄印都不一样，他只要一看蹄印就知道是什么兽。仓颉由

炎黄二帝塑像

Stone statue of Yellow Emperor and Yan Emperor

Banquan is regarded as modern day Shaanxi or Henan. The Yellow Emperor and Chiyou battled in Zhuolu and the Yellow Emperor won a big victory. Zhuolu is in the middle of Hebei today. The Yellow Emperor once reached the sea to the east, offered sacrifices of heaven and earth at Mount Taishan and reached Xiang to the south, which is currently Hunan today. The Yellow Emperor once created an ancient pot at the foot of Mount Jingshan. Now there are the remains of the ancient pot which was cast by the Yellow Emperor in Mount Jingshan, Lingbao City, Henan Province. The Yellow Emperor also once climbed the five mountains of Taishan, Taishi, Huashan, Shoushan and Donglai, where he was inspired by the heavens. These mountains are mostly located in Shaanxi, Henan and Shandong provinces.

There are many folk stories about early ancestors' lives around Zhengzhou during the period of the Yellow Emperor. In ancient times, it was said that the Yellow Emperor and Yan Emperor discarded their past grievances to make alliances, and finally the two tribes merged into the Yanhuang tribe. They jointly developed the Central Plains, erected and built houses, and gradually became rich and strong. Chiyou, the tribe leader of the southeastern regions, was violent and offensive. He heard that the Central Plains was a land of treasure, and then plundered the Central Plains. The Yellow Emperor organized the Yanhuang tribes to fight against Chiyou. It was mid-autumn, the night was cold and the day was hot. The area was always blanketed in fog, so the Yellow Emperor often lost his way in battle, and the war frequently led to frustration. In order to defeat Chiyou, the Yellow Emperor explored and visited a lot of sites and finally found a magnet stone that could be used as a direction tool, now known as a compass. Based on this tool, he made a wooden man with a magnet arm, and he made the wooden man's five fingers always pointing to the south. He named it "Fang", which means direction. He also produced a coach. The round wheels could be rotated under the wide flat board. The armrests were installed in the front, which was called "Xuan". Two wooden bars were installed in the front in order to pull the coach, which was called "Yuan". The Yellow Emperor named it "Xuanyuan Fang", which was regarded as the first mechanic tool at that time. The Yellow Emperor used it to determine the direction and finally defeated Chiyou. This folklore story is circulated in the present Xinzheng areas.

There is also a legend of Cangjie's creation of Chinese characters that reflects the certain historical facts of the Yellow Emperor's period. There were no written words

此受到启发：世上万物各有特征，抓住特征，画出图像，不就是字吗？于是他留意观察各种事物，造出了山河湖海、日月星云、树木花草、鸟兽虫鱼等很多字，从此中国有了文字。后人为纪念仓颉造字的功劳，把仓颉造字的高台叫“凤凰衔书台”，宋朝人又在这里建寺筑塔，称为“凤台寺”。现在新郑市南关有座凤台寺，相传是古代仓颉造字的地方。这个美丽的传说，流传于郑州市郊区、新郑、新密、登封一带。

现代考古研究也能证明郑州地区曾是黄帝部族活动的中心，西山遗址的发现为我们提供了充分的证据。西山古城距今 5 520 年到 4 820 年，也就是公元前 3500 年到公元前 2800 年，属黄帝时代的晚期。现代考古学研究认为，黄帝部族生活在新石器时代的晚期，即仰韶文化和龙山文化相接连的时期。1993 年，考古工作者在郑州西北邙岭的余脉上发现了一座古城遗址。这个遗址北边离黄河有 4 000 米，南北长 350 米，东西宽约 300 米，总面积大约有 10 万平方米。城中布局合理，居住区和墓葬区分开。东部的房基呈成片分布，南北成排，左右相邻，单间面积约有 30—40 平方米，呈长方形。房中有牺牲物，这说明建房前要先祭祀。

大河村遗址博物馆

The Dahe Village Ruins

in ancient times, and people kept tallies by tying knots in ropes. After the Yellow Emperor unified China, he demanded the minister Cangjie to create the characters. Then Cangjie built a house on a high platform on the south bank of the Weishui River, and focused on making characters. For a long time, Cangjie was very anxious and didn't make any characters. One day he was sitting in front of the hut thinking about creating characters and saw a phoenix that squawked and flew in the sky. A leaf fell from the phoenix's mouth. On the leaf, there was an obvious beast hoof print. An old hunter said that that was a hoof print of the beast Xiu. The hoof prints of various beasts are different. He could distinguish the beasts by their hoof print. Cangjie was inspired by this: everything in the world has its own characteristics. If we grasp features and draw images, the characters would be created. He paid attention to various things and created many words for mountains, rivers, lakes, the sun and moon, trees, flowers, birds, beasts, and so on. From that point, Chinese characters were created. In order to commemorate the merits of Cangjie's creation of characters, the descendants named the high platform "Phoenix Book Stand", and the people in the Song Dynasty built a temple and a tower there named "Fengtai Temple". Now there is a Fengtai Temple in Nanguan, Xinzheng City. It is said that it was the place where Cangjie created characters. This beautiful legend is circulated in the suburbs of Zhengzhou, Xinzheng, Xinmi and Dengfeng.

Modern archaeological studies can also prove that Zhengzhou was once the center of the tribal activities during the Yellow Emperor's period. The discovery of the Xishan site also provided us with sufficient evidence. The ancient city of Xishan formed from 3500 BC to 2800 BC, 5,520 to 4,820 years ago, which was the late period of Yellow Emperor. According to modern archaeological studies, the Yellow Emperor tribe lived in the late Neolithic period, which was the connection between the late Yangshao culture and Longshan culture. In 1993 AD, archaeologists discovered an ancient city site near the mountain side of Mount Mangshan, northwest of Zhengzhou. The ancient site is 4 kilometers away north of the Yellow River. The length is about 350 meters from north to south, and the width is about 300 meters from east to west, with a total area of about 100,000 square meters. The layout of the city is calculated reasonably. The residential area and the tomb areas are separated. In the east the houses are distributed in large quantities and organized in rows, adjacent to each other. The single room houses are shaped in rectangles which

城墙的墙基宽8—10米，城外还有5—7.5米深的壕沟，可见其有防洪和防御敌人的功能。城墙的建筑采用小板夯筑法，这种方法具有开创性的意义，在世界上也别具特色。

西山古城存在有500年左右，即从公元前3500年到公元前3000年，这一时间段恰好与黄帝时代相符。这一古城也在有熊国的区域，可见郑州地区就是黄帝部族活动的中心。黄帝在郑州地区的活动，为我们留下了许多文化遗迹。著名的大型文化遗址大河村、青台、秦王寨、点军台都在西山遗址周围，大河村遗址甚至距离西山古城不足10公里。我们可以想象，当时这些遗址中的先民就是以西山古城为他们的都城的。

中国许多有关黄帝的典籍中，都把黄帝描绘成开创文明的圣人。郑州地区仰韶文化遗址的发掘也充分证明，黄帝时代创造的灿烂文化足以代表中华文明的曙光。遗址中出土有数以万计的陶器，其中炊具占30%以上，有釜、鼎、甑、盆、钵、盘、碗、澄滤器等。这些器具可以蒸煮、烧烤、烙焙，功能多样。历史中记载有“黄帝造火食”“黄帝始造釜甑”“黄帝始蒸谷为饭”等史实，这些出土的实物具体、丰富、直接地为我们展示了黄帝时代人们的生活状态。郑州青台仰韶文化遗址中出土有距今5 500—5 000年的炭化纺织品，有麻布，也有丝绸。历史典籍中记载黄帝时有了服饰，而且养蚕缫丝，有了纺织品，还说是黄帝的妻子嫘祖教民养蚕缫丝。这些记载都与考古发掘出的实物相一致。

黄帝的事业以郑州为中心，进而辐射整个中原地区，考古发掘出的许多文化遗址都可以说明这一点。这些地区目前已知的仰韶文化和龙山文化遗址多达上千处。典籍中关于“黄帝”的解释，有一种是这样的：黄是中和之色，自然之姓，万世不易。由于黄帝创造了各种各样的制度，使得人与人、人和自然之间都能够和谐相处，所以人们尊称其为“黄帝”。中国传统文化认为黄为土，土在五行里恰好居中，所以黄帝所活动的地区就被称为“中原”“中国”。

郑州地区的先民们，首先由原始氏族社会走向早期国家阶段，有力

are about 30-40 square meters. Sacrifices were made before building each house. The city wall is about 8-10 meters thick, and there are 5-7.5 meters of trenches outside the city. This construction style functions as flood control and defense against the enemy.The construction of the city wall adopts the small-plate construction method. This method has a pioneering significance. In the world, this method is special and unique.

The ancient city of Xishan has existed for about 500 years, from 3500 BC to 3000 BC. This period coincides with the Yellow Emperor era, and this ancient city is also in the city of Youxiong. So Zhengzhou could be regarded as the center of activity during the Yellow Emperor tribe. The activities of Yellow Emperor in the Zhengzhou region left us with many cultural relics. The famous large-scale cultural sites, such as Dahe Village, Qingtai, Qinwangzhai and Dianjuntai, are all around the Xishan site. The Dahe Village Ruins is even less than 10 kilometers away from the ancient city of Xishan. We can imagine that the ancient city of Xishan was their capital for these cultural relics.

In many ancient books of China, the Yellow Emperor was described as a saint and a pioneer of China's civilization. The excavation of the Yangshao Cultural Ruins in Zhengzhou also fully proves that the splendid culture created during the Yellow Emperor period is enough to represent the dawn of Chinese civilization. Tens of thousands of pottery were discovered at the site, of which more than 30% was cookware. The types of cookware found at the site included kettles, tripods, basins, pots, plates, bowl and filters. These utensils were used to cook, grill, bake and had a variety of other functions. In history, there were such facts as "the Yellow Emperor created cooking", "the Yellow Emperor created and designed the pot" and "the Yellow Emperor steamed rice to eat". The people learned these things from the Yellow Emperor. These unearthed objects directly inform us about the lifestyle people had during the Yellow Emperor period. In the Yangshao cultural ruins, carbonized textiles, including linen and silk which were made 5,500-5,000 years ago, were unearthed in Qingtai, Zhengzhou. In the historical records, people had clothes during the Yellow Emperor's reign, and they raised silkworms and made textiles. It was also said that the wife of the Yellow Emperor taught the people how to raise silkworm and how to make silk. These records are consistent with the material objects excavated by archaeology.

黄帝故里
Hometown of the Yellow Emperor

地促进了中华民族早期文化的发展。国家首先在这一地区形成，古都也首先在这一地区建立起来，中国古都学会会长史念海为新郑黄帝故里题词“中华第一古都”。可见郑州在中国古都史上的开创性作用。

## 第二节 禹都阳城，治水为民

大禹治水的故事在中国几乎家喻户晓，大禹“三过家门而不入”的事迹激励着我们公而忘私、先人后己。大禹其实是中国第一个统一的奴隶制王朝夏朝的奠基者，他的儿子启是夏朝的第一位君主。夏朝的建立，是一件具有革命性意义的大事，它表明中华民族已经迈向了文明社会。大禹是中华民族史前传说的最后一位领袖人物，他的形象非常平民化，是一位手持木耒的健壮的劳动者。他带领先民治理水患的事迹，流传了数千年，成为中华民族艰苦奋斗精神的源头，他的事迹永远闪耀着不朽的光辉。司马迁的《史记》里说大禹的父亲叫鲧，鲧的父亲是颛顼，颛顼的父亲叫昌意，昌意的父亲就是黄帝。这表明大禹就是黄帝的后裔，

Zhengzhou was the center of the Yellow Emperor's career, and then extended to the Central Plains, which could be proven by many archaeology discoveries. Now there are thousands of Yangshao culture and Longshan cultural ruins in these areas. In ancient records and books, one of the explanations about the name of "Yellow Emperor" is like this: yellow is the color of neutrality, the essence of nature, and it will never fade away. Because the Yellow Emperor created a variety of rules and policies, people were able to live harmoniously with nature. In order to show respect to him, people addressed him as "Yellow Emperor". According to traditional Chinese culture, yellow is the colour of soil. The soil is right in the middle of the Five Elements. Therefore, the area where the Yellow Emperor conducted government activities is called the "Central Plains" or "Middle Kingdom—China".

The early society in the area of Zhengzhou evolved from a primitive clan into an early nation. This society effectively promoted the development of early Chinese culture. The new country was formed here first and then the ancient capital was established. Shi Nianhai, the former chairman of Chinese Ancient Capital Association wrote an inscription of "The First Ancient Capital in China" for Xinzheng—the Yellow Emperor's hometown. This showed the pioneering role of Zhengzhou in the history of ancient Chinese capitals.

## II. The Legend of Yu: Flood Control in Yangcheng

The story of Yu controlling the flood is widely known in China. People are impressed by his selfless spirit that passing his own home three times without entering so that he could help others before entering his own home to rebuild. In fact Yu was the founder of the first unified slavery dynasty—Xia in China. His son Qi was the first monarch in Xia Dynasty. The establishment of the Xia Dynasty is a revolutionary event. It shows that Chinese society has moved towards a civilized society. Yu is the last leader of the prehistoric legends of the Chinese people. He was imaged as a civilian-style strong labourer with a raft. He led the people and controlled the floods. The story has been passed down for thousands of years, and this story became the source of the Chinese people's spirit of hard work. His deeds will always shine with immortal brilliance. Sima Qian's *Shi Ji* (*Records of the Historian*) said that Yu's father was called Gun, Gun's father was called Zhuanxu, Zhuanxu's

部落联盟的领袖就是这样一代代更替的。

中国古籍上说“禹都阳城”，又说“禹避舜之子于阳城”，这说明大禹的都城就是阳城。阳城在哪里？阳城就在嵩山脚下，就是现在郑州市所辖登封市的告成镇。

20 世纪 80 年代初，考古工作者在告成镇附近的王城岗发现了两座城堡遗迹。经分析，这两处遗址代表着龙山文化晚期和二里头文化早期，也就是距今 4 400 年左右的先夏文化。两城东西并列，面积约 1 万平方米。城中除了出土有青铜器残片外，还有陶片，上面刻有文字，颇似“共”字。城中有房基的遗迹，没有大型的宫室，生活用品等非常俭朴，但是祭祀的建筑却非常明显。在历史记载中，大禹非常俭朴，对于个人的衣食住行等极不讲究，但是对于祭祀等事却非常看重。从城中的发现来看，历史记载还是有一定可信度的。

现在的告成镇东北有一处遗址，就是古代的阳城，也可以说古代的

禹都阳城

Yangcheng, the capital city of Yu

father was called Changyi and Changyi's father was called the Yellow Emperor. This shows that Yu was a descendant of the Yellow Emperor. Tribe leaders were determined through this lineage.

In ancient Chinese books, it was said that Yangcheng was the capital city of Yu's tribe. There was another saying that Yu escaped to Yangcheng in order to avoid Shun's son. So we could infer that the capital of Yu's tribe was Yangcheng. Where is Yangcheng? Yangcheng is at the foot of Mount Songshan, located in today's Gaocheng Town in Dengfeng City, which is under the jurisdiction of Zhengzhou City.

In the early 1980s, archaeologists discovered two castle ruins in Wangchenggang, near Gaocheng Town. After analysis, the two ruins originated from the late Longshan culture and the early Erlitou culture, which was regarded as the beginning of Xia Dynasty culture around 4,400 years ago. The two ruins were situated in a line from east to west, with an area of about 10,000 square meters. Besides bronze fragments, pottery pieces were also discovered at the two sites, which were engraved with the Chinese character "Gong". There were relics of the houses and the daily necessities. There was no palace, but the architecture for sacrifice was very easy to identify. According to the historical records, Yu was very thrifty, and he never paid much attention to his clothes, food, accommodation, etc. However, he valued sacrifices. From the discovery at the two ruins, we could infer that the historical records still have some credibility.

In the northeast of Gaocheng there is a historical relic, which was the city of Yangcheng in the ancient time. Or we can say that ancient Yangcheng is today's Gaocheng Town. The site is about 2,000 meters long from north to south and 700 meters wide from east to west. There are regular urban water supply and drainage facilities. Some pottery beans, measurements and kettles were also found, which the Chinese characters "Yangcheng Warehouse" or "Yangcheng" were printed. These cultural relics fully prove that this was the location of ancient Yangcheng. The name of Yangcheng had been used since the Spring and Autumn Period and the Warring States Period. It was changed to Gaocheng County in the reign of Empress Wu Zetian of the Tang Dynasty.

The story of "Qimu Stone" about Yu is popular in Dengfeng. In ancient times, people always suffered losses caused by floods. In order to let people live and work in

阳城就是今天的告成镇。这处遗址南北长约 2 000 米，东西宽 700 米，有规整的城市供排水设施，也发现了一些陶豆、量、釜等器具，上面印有非常明显的“阳城仓器”“阳城”这样的字眼，这就完全证明了这就是古代的阳城。阳城这个名字在春秋战国时也一直沿用，一直到唐代武则天时才改为告成县。

现在登封一带还流传着一个启母石的故事。古时候洪水横流，为了让人民安居乐业，大禹治水踏遍了九州。在嵩山南面，西自龙门，东到禹县（今河南省禹州市），有一条大河叫颍河，颍河一泛滥，两岸就变成一片汪洋，什么庄稼也不能生长。大禹为了把洪水排出去，就在登封市西北的萼岭口一带凿山治水，打算把嵩山南面的洪水引进北面的洛河，然后再让它流到黄河里去。这一天，大禹来到萼岭口附近一看，这里山势险峻，凿通萼岭口工程很大。他为了快些开通河道，在凿山时就变成一只巨大的黑熊。大禹每天忙着开山凿石，没工夫回家，也顾不上吃饭，就叫妻子涂山氏给他送饭。他为了不让妻子知道自己变熊的事，就跟妻子约定，只要她听见敲鼓的声音就去给他送饭。涂山氏也非常支持他的工作，每天当听到咚咚的鼓声时，她就赶快撑着木筏子，把饭给大禹送到开山的工地上去。这样，夫妻两人虽说都很辛苦，但心里却很高兴。

有一天，大禹在山坡上行走的时候一不留心，脚下踩动的几块石头从山上滚了下来，刚好掉在鼓面上，发出了“咚咚”的响声。大禹因为忙，走得急，也没在意，只管自己上山去了。涂山氏一听到鼓声，心里纳闷，今天丈夫为什么吃饭早了呢？她也没有多想，赶紧把饭做好，急急忙忙撑着木筏子就给大禹送饭去了。她来到山坡前，左等右等也不见大禹回来，就往山上爬去。她来到山上往下一看，只见有一头大黑熊正在山下用力凿石推土、开挖河道。它伸出两条巨臂，用力朝山岩上一推，只听“轰隆”一声响，山石塌下了一大片，倒在水里，溅起几丈高的浪花。大黑熊这才直起腰来，看看新开出来的山口，乐得眉开眼笑。涂山氏一见，大吃一惊，心想：自己的丈夫大禹，怎么是一只大黑熊呀？平时自

peace, Yu tried every means to control the flood all over the country. On the south of Mount Songshan, there was a river named Yinghe, which flowed from Longmen in the west to Yu County (now Yuzhou city, Henan province) in the east. Once Yinghe River flooded, the banks became like the vast sea and no crops could grow there. In order to release the flood waters, Yu drilled holes in the mountain near Elingkou in the northwest of Dengfeng. He attempted to release the flood from the south of the Mount Songshan to the north of the Luohe River, and then let it flow into the Yellow River. One day Yu went to Elingkou and saw the steep mountains and realized that it would be a huge project. In order to build the watercourses quickly, he transformed into a huge black bear when he was digging the mountains. Yu was too busy digging in the mountains every day to have meals at home, so he asked his wife Tushan to deliver the food to him. In order not to let his wife know that he transformed into a bear, he made an appointment with his wife. Only when hearing the sound of drumming, she would deliver the food to him. His wife, Tushan, also gave a lot of support to his work. Every day, when she heard the sound of drums, she pulled the wooden raft and sent food for him to the construction site. Although life for them was very hard, they were very happy.

One day, Yu walked up the hill and accidentally stepped on a stone which fell down a hill and hit the drum. Because he was engaged in other things, he didn't pay attention to that, and went to the mountain directly. When Tushan heard the drums, she wondered why her husband wanted to have a meal so early today. She didn't think much about it and quickly prepared the meal and sent the food by the wooden boat. After arriving at the foot of the hill, she waited for a long time, but she didn't see her husband. Then she began to climb the mountain. When she climbed the hill and looked down, she saw a big black bear, which was digging in the mountain and excavating the watercourse. The bear stretched out two giant arms and pushed the rocks with much effort, making a loud noise causing the rocks to fall into the river. The big black bear just straightened up and looked at the newly opened mountain pass, smiling. At the sight of the scene, Tushan was shocked. She thought, "My husband couldn't be a big black bear! Why couldn't I see that before?" At that time she didn't know what to do. She grabbed the basket and ran home quickly. On the way home, she was ashamed and anxious. When she arrived at her home, she felt sorrow. She stood there and turned into a stone. Yu came to the drum at noon and

己为什么没有发现呢？一时间，她不知道怎么办才好，就提起饭篮赶快往家跑。一路上，她又羞又急又气。当快到家门口时，她心里一阵难过，往那里一站，就变成了一块石头。再说大禹，他晌午时来到大鼓跟前敲起鼓来，可是，他敲敲，等等，等等，敲敲，好久也不见妻子送饭来。他想一定是出了事，就赶紧往家走。

大禹回到家里，里里外外找不着妻子的影子，只见家门口的山坡上多了一块巨大的岩石，旁边还放着饭篮子。大禹这才明白，原来妻子已经变成岩石了。这时，大禹后悔不该把自己变熊的事瞒着妻子。他又想：妻子已经怀孕很久了，这一来，咋办呢？我没有儿子，谁继承我的治水大业呢？想到这里，他就急匆匆地走到巨石前面，大声喊道："孩子他娘啊！你就这样离开我了吗？你要把儿子交给我呀！"突然，"轰隆"一声响，这块巨大的岩石裂开了，跳出一个孩子，大禹急忙把儿子抱了起来。后来，大禹给这个孩子起名字叫启，那块巨石就叫"启母石"。

现在，登封市嵩山脚下矗立着一块巨大的石头，像一尊雕像站立在

登封启母石

Qimu Stone in Dengfeng

played the drum, waiting for a long time, but his wife didn't show up. He guessed that something happened and hurried home.

When Yu returned home, he looked everywhere, but he didn't find his wife. He could only see a huge rock on the hillside by his house and a basket next to it. Yu realized that his wife turned into a rock. At that time Yu felt regret that he didn't tell his wife the truth. He thought, "My wife was pregnant for a period of time. So what should I do now? I have no son, so who will inherit my career of water control?" When he thought of it, he walked to the front of the stone and shouted, "My dear! How can you leave me alone? You should give me a son!" Suddenly, there was a crash of thunder, and a little boy jumped out from the huge stone. Yu immediately hugged his son. Later, he named his son Qi. Therefore, the stone was given a name "Qimu Stone".

Now, there is a huge stone standing at the foot of Mount Songshan in Dengfeng City, shaped like a woman. It is called the "Qimu Stone", according to the legend. Not far from the "Qimu Stone", there are two pillars which were made of large square stones. On the pillars were carved inscriptions which showed hunting and farming. This is considered the door of Yu's house. People called it "Qimu Door".

## III. The Capital of the Shang Dynasty:Bo

When Yu's son established the Xia Dynasty, he appointed states by royalty. One of the states was the Shang kingdom. The leader of this state was called Xie, and Xie helped Yu to control the water. He was appointed to own the state of Shang by royalty. The totem of state Shang is called Black Bird. An interesting story goes that a black bird gave birth to Shang. It is said that the second concubine of the emperor Ku, Jian Di, who was the daughter of Yourong, saw a bird's egg when she went out to take a bath with her friends. Jiandi swallowed the egg and was pregnant, then gave birth to Xie. Later, Xie did a lot of good things for the people and was honored as the ancestor of the Shang people. The Black Bird is an ancient name for the swallow. Because the swallow is black, it was given such name. At that time both the black bird and phoenix referred to the swallow. From the story about Xie's mother giving birth to him after eating the swallow's egg, ancient people have known that swallows build a nest in the middle of spring to lay eggs. Shang people thought that the arrival

那里，相传这就是“启母石”。在离“启母石”不远的地方，还立着两根由大块方石头垒成的门柱，上边刻着打猎、农耕的浮雕画，这就是当时大禹的家门口，后人叫“启母阙”。

## 第三节 商汤都亳，奠定基业

大禹的儿子夏启建国时，分封了一些诸侯，其中有一个商国，这个部族的首领叫契，他协助大禹治水有功，就被封于商地。商部族的图腾是玄鸟，中国古代典籍上说“天命玄鸟，降而生商”，这里面还有一个有趣的故事。据说，帝喾的次妃简狄是有戎氏的女儿，与闺中好友外出洗澡时看到一枚鸟蛋。简狄吞下鸟蛋后，怀孕生下了契。契后来为民做了许多好事，被尊为商人的始祖。“玄鸟”是古人对燕子的称呼，因燕子通体黑色，故名“玄鸟”。当时，玄鸟、凤都是指燕子。关于商人的祖先契是其母吞燕子卵而生之事，我们也可以这样来理解：春分时节，燕子筑巢生子。商人以为燕子来临便是繁殖的好日子，于是，在燕子来临的仲春之时，夫妻双双赴郊外旷野之地举行求子祭祀活动，这个时期所孕之子，谓之“玄鸟所生”。

商这个部族农业很发达，生产工具很先进，也非常重视贸易，这样他们的农业和商业就很快地发展了起来。我们现在常说的一个词语“商人”就是起源于商这个部族，说的是他们非常会做生意。他们曾经发明牛车，用于长距离运输货物，节省人力。商部族有了实力，就不断地向外扩展，一步步侵削夏王朝的诸侯方国，扩大自己的地盘。到了夏王朝的末年，这时夏的国君叫桀，他非常残暴，失尽了民心，民众指着太阳来骂他：“你什么时候灭亡啊，我愿意和你一起灭亡。”民众连夏桀的名字都不愿意提了，可见这个夏王是多么不得民心！商部族的领袖叫汤，他很能干，亲自去做许多大大小小的事情，给大家树立了勤奋努力的好榜样。同时，他还很会用人，把许多有品德有能力的人都团结到自己身

of the swallow was a good day for breeding. Therefore, around the spring equinox, when the swallows arrived, both husband and wife went to the wilderness to hold a sacrificial service to promote fertility. If the wife was pregnant at this time, that was called "the birth of the Black Bird".

Agriculture was very well developed during the Shang Dynasty. People used advanced production tools. They paid much attention to the agriculture and business, which also developed quickly. Nowadays we have a word "businessman", which originated from the Shang Tribe. The word "businessman" means a person who is good at doing business. They invented cattle carts for long-distance transportation by which the goods were shipped and man's labour was saved. Because the Shang tribe became strong, they continued to expand outward. They invaded the countries of the Xia Dynasty step-by-step to enlarge their own territory. At the end of the Xia Dynasty, when the King Jie came to the throne, he was very cruel and lost the hearts of the people. The people pointed at the sun and cursed him. Among the people there was a saying like this, "If you are going to perish, I am willing to die with you." In people's heart, he was such a bad king that no one would like to talk about him. The leader of the Shang tribe was called Tang. He was very capable. He had done many things and set a good example of hard working for the people. At the same time, he was very good at choosing people. He gathered a lot of people who had good morality and ability. Among them there was a man called Yi Yin. This man was very clever and had a great talent in politics and economy. He had a strong standing in the society. According to historical records, Yi Yin gathered a large number of people to make splendid clothes and then sold the clothes to the bureaucrats of the Xia Dynasty. On one hand, Yi Yin increased his own tribe's income and used the money to purchase some of war materials. On the other hand, through this exchange, the rulers of the Xia Dynasty became more extravagant and corrupt. The rulers had no fighting spirit, so Yi Yin thus gained the initiative of war. When the people of the Xia Dynasty could no longer stand the ruler Jie, Shang Tang led the army to attack the Xia Dynasty, which collapsed quickly. Since then a new era of Shang Dynasty began with the capital in Bo.

The ruins of the ancient city of Shang are inside of modern Zhengzhou City, among Chengdong Road, Chengnan Road, Jinshui Road and Duling Street. Shang City was regarded as the early capital city Bo. For 150 years there were 10 kings

边，其中就有一位叫伊尹。这个人聪明得很，很有政治经济才能，眼光看得非常长远。根据史书记载，伊尹发动民众缝制大量的锦绣衣服，然后卖给夏王朝的官僚贵族。这样一方面可以增加自己的收入，购进一些战争所需的物资，另一方面也可以让夏王朝的统治者们更加奢侈腐化，精神松懈，没有斗志，从而取得战争的主动权。等到夏王朝的民众再也无法忍受夏桀的统治了，这时商汤率领军队向夏朝发起了进攻，夏王朝一下子就崩溃了。商朝从此建立起来，商汤在亳地建立都城，开始了中国历史上又一个新的王朝。

郑州商城遗址位于现在的郑州市内，大约在城东路、城南路、金水路、杜岭街之间。郑州商城是商代的前期都城亳都，从商汤至太戊共历经 10 个王，约 150 年。郑州西北郊小双桥村还有一个商代都城遗址，据专家考证，这是商代中期的隞都。小双桥遗址作为商代中期仲丁的国都，大约有 20 年。之后，这个地方仍然不时作为后来的商王的国都使用。综合起来，郑州作为商代国都的时间应在 200 年左右。

郑州商城的建立非常具有战略眼光，可见商汤为了推翻夏王朝的统治，是下了一番功夫的。从军事上来说，它西边距离夏王朝都城不到 100 千米，战争发生时，商汤能够很快召集军队，对夏王朝形成包围之势。从自然地理位置上来说，郑州是一个理想的建都地方。郑州地势平坦，土地肥沃，西边与北边主要是丘陵地带，城内外有金水河、熊耳河、荥泽、圃田泽等，可以说是一个依山傍水、可攻可守的地方。

郑州商城，具有内城和外郭，功能比较完备，其内外城遗址总面积达到 25 平方千米。内城基本上依照正南北和正东西修建，四周均由夯土围合起来。北城墙长约 1 690 米，西墙长约 1 870 米，南墙和东墙长度均为 1 700 米，东西南北四段城墙总长 6 960 米，城墙底部宽度一般为 20—25 米，顶宽 5 米多，现存城墙最高为 9 米。外城指的是内城外面修建的又一道防御体系。现在的南关外有一段外城墙，总长度在 3 000 米以上，西面的外城约在今福寿街与解放路相交处，城墙全由人工夯筑

from King Tang to King Taiwu. There is another Shang City ruin in Xiaoshuangqiao Village in the northwest suburb of Zhengzhou. According to the experts, this was the second capital city Ao. Xiaoshuangqiao site was the capital of Zhongding during the middle term of the Shang Dynasty for about 20 years. Later this place often served as the capital of the Shang Dynasty. As a result, Zhengzhou served as a capital of the Shang Dynasty for about 200 years.

The establishment of Zhengzhou Shang City was very strategic, from which we can see that Shang Tang had made some efforts to overthrow the rule of the Xia Dynasty. From a military perspective, Shang City was less than 100 kilometers west of the capital city of the Xia Dynasty. When the war broke out, Shang Tang was able to quickly launch an army and form a siege of the Xia Dynasty. From a natural geographical point of view, Zhengzhou was an ideal place to build capital because it was situated on a flat, fertile land with hills in the west and north. There were the Jinshui River, Xiong'er River, Yingze and Putianze in and around the city. It can be said that it is a good place for attack and defense with the mountains and waters nearby.

Zhengzhou Shang City site had an inner city and an outer city, and its functions were relatively complete. The total area of its inner and outer city sites reached 25 square kilometers. The inner city was basically built in accordance with the north and south, west and east, and was surrounded by soil. The north city wall is about 1,690 meters long, while the west wall is about 1,870 meters long. The south wall and the east wall are both 1,700 meters long. The total length of the four sections is 6,960 meters. The width of the bottom of the wall is generally 20-25 meters. The height of the city wall is more than 5 meters, and the existing highest part is about 9 meters. The outer city refers to another defense system built outside the inner city. There is a part of outer city wall near Nanguan with a total length of more than 3,000 meters. The outer city to the west is at the intersection of today's Fushou Street and Jiefang Road. The walls were all handmade. When we calculate length, width and height of the walls, some people roughly estimate that there were 870 thousand cubic meters of soil for the construction of Zhengzhou Shang City. Before construction, the digging work reached 1,740 thousand cubic meters. This was a huge project in the world at that time, which also showed the great momentum of the Shang Dynasty's capital. When defeating the Xia Dynasty, Shang Tang wanted to build an extraordinary

郑州商代遗址
Shang Dynasty Ruins in Zhengzhou

而成。有人粗略地估算过，以全部的城墙长、宽、高计算，郑州商城约用夯土量为 87 万立方米，夯前挖土量约 174 万立方米。这在当时世界是十分浩大的工程，也从一个侧面说明了商朝都城的气势。我们可以想象，当年商汤灭夏胜利返回后，一定想把自己的王都建造得气派非凡，那些战俘们正好可以充当筑城的民工，商王朝粮仓里的粮食正好可以作为这个庞大的筑城群体的口粮。郑州商城的内城中还有一个贵族的宫殿区，它位于郑州商城内中部偏东和东北部一带，总面积约 40 万平方米，这样的建筑规模在 3 600 年前是非常罕见的。它的边沿处有夯土城墙、石制水槽、水管和壕沟等。石制水槽长 100 米，宽 20 米，水槽壁用圆石头加固，底部铺有规整的青灰色石板，表面还铺有料礓石。在宫殿区内还发现了多处大型宫室的房基和柱础槽，此外还发现了青铜簪、玉簪，还有一些被锯割过的奴隶头骨。郑州商城出土有许多青铜器，其大多不是随墓葬出土，而是从窖藏中出土。其中有一件铜方鼎高达 1 米，口径长 0.61—0.625 米，重约 86.4 千克，已成为郑州市的象征。其他相似重量的方鼎还有 10 余件之多。这些重大的青铜器只能是王室的器物，这

capital. The prisoners of the war were used as workers to build the walls. The food in the barn of the Shang Dynasty fed the construction workers. There is also a palace of the nobility in the inner city of Shang City. It was located in the east and northeast side of Shang City, which occupied about 400 thousand square meters. This scale of construction was very rare in the world 3,600 years ago. At the edge of the palace there were earthly walls, stone sinks, water pipes and ditches. The stone sink was 100 meters long and 20 meters wide. The wall of the sink was reinforced with round stones. The bottom was covered with grey slates and the surface was covered with pebbles. In the palace, a number of foundations and pillars of rooms were found. In addition, bronze hairpins, jade hairpins and some slaves' skulls were found. Many bronzes were unearthed in Shang City, but most of them were not found from the tombs, but from the cellars. Among them there was a rectangular cauldron which was 1 meter tall, with a dimension of 0.61 to 0.625 meters and a weight of 86.4 kilograms. It has become a symbol of Zhengzhou. There were about more than 10 cauldrons with similar height. These huge bronzes only could be used by the royal family, which showed that Zhengzhou Shang City was the capital city of the Shang Dynasty. What is worth mentioning is that a complete original green glazed porcelain statue was unearthed in an ancient tomb outside the western wall of Zhengzhou Shang City. It is 27 centimeters high and decorated with basket veins. The body was off white, delicate and hard. The surface of the porcelain was covered by yellow and green. The excavation and discovery of this porcelain has brought the history of Chinese porcelain forward to 3,500 years ago. In addition, a group of workshops and bronze wares were found in Zhengzhou Shang City. More than 300 meters away from the north city wall, it was the site of the copper-casting workshop. A bone-making workshop site was found on the north of the copper workshop. A copper-casting workshop was found about 600 meters away from the south wall, and a pottery workshop was found about 1,300 meters outside the west wall. Most of the unearthed cultural relics are pottery, bronzes, stoneware, bones, as well as mussel, jade, primitive porcelain, printed hard pottery, white pottery, and ivory.

It was said that the first king of the Shang Dynasty set his capital in Bo, which was today's Zhengzhou. He ruled the country with righteousness so the people were in support of him. The country became more and more prosperous. Unfortunately, the weather was very dry, and the country had no grain for five years. Then Shang

表明郑州商城是商代都城确定无疑。更值得一提的是，郑州商城西墙外一座古墓内出土了一件完整的原始青釉瓷尊，高 27 厘米，饰席纹和篮纹，胎质呈灰白色，细腻坚硬，器表遍施光亮晶莹的黄绿色釉，这件原始瓷尊的出土把中国的制瓷历史提前到距今 3 500 年前。此外，在郑州商城还发现一批手工业作坊遗址和铜器窖藏。北城墙外 300 多米处，为铸铜作坊遗址，在铸铜作坊遗址北部发现一处制骨作坊遗址，南城墙外约 600 米处发现一处铸铜作坊遗址，西城墙外约 1 300 米处发现一处制陶作坊遗址。出土的文物以陶器最多，青铜器、石器、骨器次之，并有蚌器、玉器、原始瓷器、印纹硬陶、白陶器、象牙器等。

传说商代开国之君成汤灭夏之后，定都于亳，也就是现在的郑州。他以仁义治国，臣民非常拥护他，国力日益强盛。不巧天气大旱，国家整整 5 年颗粒无收。商汤于是亲自在桑林中祈求降雨，他说："我一人有罪，不要殃及百姓，若百姓有罪，也由我一人承担，不要因为一人触犯了上天，而使鬼神做出伤害百姓性命的事来。"他让人搬来柴草，剪其发，磨其手，准备引火自焚，为民请命。这时，突然天降甘霖，浇灭了大火，缓解了旱灾。可见商汤对于老百姓拥有怎么样的情感，人民又怎么会不拥戴他呢？《史记》中记载着一件事，也说到商汤的为人。有一次，商汤从大禹治水为民造福说起，告诫一些追随他的官员："如果你们不时时刻刻想着百姓，不刻苦努力工作，工作成绩很少，那么我就要处罚你们，我一定说到做到。"

商汤作为一个有作为、品德好的部族首领创造了灿烂的早期历史，我们绝不能忘记像商汤这样的中华民族的先贤。

## 第四节　郑韩故都，东周名城

郑州市所辖的新郑市城区就是历史上赫赫有名的郑韩故都。由于新郑市这个地方曾经是郑国和韩国的都城，这两个国家又分别是春秋和战

Tang personally prayed for rain by a mulberry bush. He said: "I am guilty, leave the people alone. If the people are guilty, I am also responsible for it. Don't let the ghosts and Gods do something that hurts the lives of the people because one person has violated Heaven." He asked people to move firewood, cut his hair, grind his hands, preparing to set himself on fire to sacrifice himself for the people. At this time, the rain fell suddenly, the fire was extinguished, and the drought was alleviated. It could be seen that Shang Tang treated his people so well that all the people supported him. In the *Shi Ji* (*Records of the Historian*), it mentioned one thing which could explain Tang's merits. Once, when Shang Tang spoke of Yu's controlling the water, he warned his followers, "If you don't always think of the people, or don't work hard, you will be punished for your laziness and lack of ability. I will fulfill my words."

Being an excellent tribal leader, Shang Tang created brilliant early history. The great sages of the Chinese nation like Shang Tang will be remembered forever.

## IV. The Ancient Capital City of Zheng and Han in the Eastern Zhou Dynasty

The city of Xinzheng, under the jurisdiction of Zhengzhou City, was the famous capital of the state of Zheng and the state of Han in history. Ancient Zhengzhou served as the capital for Zheng and Han, the two powerful states in the Spring and Autumn Period and the Warring States Period. Xinzheng city is also known as the famous capital city in the Eastern Zhou Dynasty.

In the Western Zhou Dynasty, King Xuan of Zhou conferred the title of Duke Huan of Zheng to his younger brother. His territory was located in today's Fengxiang County, Shaanxi Province. By the end of the Western Zhou Dynasty, King You was profligate and devoid of principles. When Xirong invaded, Duke Huan of Zheng consulted with Grand Historian Shibo about moving eastward. He felt satisfied with Zhengzhou, which was located in the hinterland of the Central Plains. Specifically it referred to today's Jingxiangcheng village in the southeast of Xingyang. He moved his family and property first. Unfortunately, Duke Huan of Zheng died in the Battle of Lishan. Duke Wu of Zheng succeeded the throne and followed King Ping of Zhou move eastward to Luo. He re-established the state of Zheng and settled the capital in the hill area, which is now the Xinzheng urban area. Later, Zheng was

国时期的大国，所以新郑被称为“东周名城，郑韩故都”。

西周时，周宣王封其庶弟为郑桓公，封地原在今陕西凤翔县。到了西周末年，幽王荒淫无道，西戎入侵，郑桓公就与太史史伯共谋东迁。他看中了地处中原腹地的郑州，就先把家属和财物迁来，具体地点就在现在的荥阳东南京襄城村。谁知郑桓公在骊山战役中战死，为国捐躯。郑武公继位，跟随周平王东迁洛邑，重新建立郑国，定都于郑父之丘，也就是现在的新郑市区。后来，郑国在公元前 375 年为韩国所灭，共存在 432 年，新郑作为郑国都城有 330 年左右。

郑国都城选址较合理，在双洎河与黄水河的交汇处，能够保证城市用水的需要。宫城与手工作坊分开，一个在城的中心区，一个在城的外廓区。宫殿区位居城北，开创了中国都城中宫殿位于城的北部的先河。都城高大坚固，城阙的楼台很高，西城墙建有 4 个马面，可谓易守难攻。当年韩国攻郑，经过 10 年之久才攻下此城。秦国攻韩，也是用了几乎 10 年才攻下。

郑国都城出土的青铜器数量多、形制大，尤其以礼器和乐器为盛。考古工作者曾经一次就发掘出青铜礼器 142 件，乐器 211 件。郑国都城出土的青铜编钟，从套数和件数上看，都位居东周列国之首。史书上记载说郑国的音乐发达，这一点从出土文物上也可以得到证实。这里面最值得称道的是大型青铜器莲鹤方壶，这件青铜器物通高 1.62 米，重达 64.28 千克，可谓春秋时期青铜器物之精品。著名历史学家郭沫若一见之下就叹为精品，情不自禁地赞颂莲鹤方壶是时代精神的象征。这青铜器目前已是河南博物院的镇院之宝。东周是一个社会大变革的时代，郑国可谓是率先开启了这一伟大时代。莲鹤方壶不仅表现了郑国青铜器铸造的精美工艺，更表现了郑国打破传统、昂扬向上的精神。其实，郑国得以在春秋初期雄强一时，几乎达到“挟天子以令诸侯”的地步，就是因为大胆变革、不拘旧礼的观念。

郑国初期的一位英主郑庄公就是一位不拘传统的人。他假借周王的

destroyed by Han in 375 BC. Zheng existed for 432 years, and Xinzheng served as the capital city for about 330 years.

The location of the capital city of Zheng was very reasonable. It was at the intersection of Shuangji River and the Yellow River, with a guaranteed water supply. The palace and craft workshops were separated. One was in the middle of the city and the other was out of the city. The palace area was located in the north of the city, which set an example for the location of the palace on the north of the capital in Chinese history. The city walls of the capital were high and strong. The Gate Que towers were also high. The west city walls had four balconies, which were easy to defend and difficult to attack. When Han attacked Zheng, it took them 10 years to conquer the city. When Qin attacked Han, it also took them almost 10 years to conquer the city.

The number of bronzes unearthed in the capital of Zheng were large and the shape was also large. Most of them were ritual instruments and musical instruments. Archaeologists once discovered 142 bronze rituals and 211 musical instruments. The bronze bells unearthed in the capital of Zheng are ranked first among the kingdoms in the Eastern Zhou Dynasty, both in terms of the number of sets and the number of pieces. The history book states that music in Zheng was developed, and this could be confirmed from the unearthed cultural relics. The most commendable bronze was the Lotus Crane Square Pot, which was 1.62 meters high and 64.28 kilograms in weight. This could be regarded as a boutique of the bronze wares during the Spring and Autumn Period. The famous historian Guo Moruo praised at first sight that the Lotus Crane Square Pot was a symbol of the spirit of the times. This bronze is now the treasure of the Henan Museum. The Eastern Zhou Dynasty was an era of great social change. Zheng could be said to be the first to open this great era. The Lotus Crane Square Pot not only showed the exquisite craftsmanship of Zheng but also showed Zheng's spirit of breaking the tradition. In fact, Zheng was so powerful in the early period of the Spring and Autumn Period that it could order all lords by holding the emperor in power, which was due to its bold reform and social changes.

In the early period of the state of Zheng, Duke Zhuang of Zheng was an unconventional person. In the name of King Zhou, he attacked the state of Song, personally brought troops to invade the State of Wei, and attacked the states of Xu and Chen. He even dared to harvest the wheat which belonged to the Zhou royal

莲鹤方壶
Lotus Crane Square Pot

名义，兴师伐宋，亲自带兵侵略卫国，攻打许国和陈国，甚至敢去收割属于周王室的麦子。当时周王势力衰微，为了缓和与郑国的关系，不得不屈尊和郑国互相派遣人质。郑庄公在对待自己母亲这件事上，也表现得异于常人。郑庄公弟兄二人，他的母亲武姜非常宠爱弟弟共叔段。为了让共叔段当上国君，武姜千方百计地为共叔段争取利益。等到共叔段势力大了后，武姜就做内应，让共叔段谋反，推翻郑庄公的统治，自己取而代之。谁知这一切都被郑庄公看在眼里，记在心里，等到共叔段起兵后，他一举就消灭了共叔段的军队，共叔段最后迫不得已自杀了。郑庄公从此对他的母亲非常反感，扬言“我和母亲不到黄泉不再见面”。但是亲情终究无法割断，时间一长，郑庄公就有些后悔了。这时，颍考叔建议他挖地道与母亲相见，以慰相思之情。当地道挖好，郑庄公与武姜再一次相见时，郑庄公一下子紧紧地抱住了母亲。这就是著名的“掘地见母”的故事。

family. At that time, King Zhou's power declined. In order to ease the relationship with Zheng, he had to agree to send hostages to each other. Duke Zhuang of Zheng also behaved differently with ordinary people in how to treat his mother. Duke Zhuang of Zheng had a brother called Gongshuduan, who was spoiled by their mother Wu Jiang. In order to let Gongshuduan be a monarch, Wu Jiang tried every means to fight for his interests. Wu Jiang planned to help Gongshuduan from the inside, and let him rebel in order to overthrow the rule of Duke Zhuang of Zheng. Wu Jiang wanted her son Gongshuduan to overthrow his older brother and be the king, but Duke Zhuang of Zheng knew the plan. Duke Zhuang of Zheng wiped out Gongshuduan's army. Gongshuduan was forced to commit suicide. Duke Zhuang of Zheng was very disgusted with his mother after Gongshuduan's rebellion. Duke Zhuang of Zheng said that "My mother and I won't meet until we die". However, the family relationship could not be cut off. Duke Zhuang of Zheng felt regret after a period. At this time, Ying Kaoshu suggested that he dig tunnels to meet his mother to express his affection. When the tunnel was finished, Duke Zhuang of Zheng and Wu Jiang met again. Duke Zhuang of Zheng hugged his mother tightly. This was the famous story named "digging the tunnel to see the mother".

After a few hundred years, Zheng was no longer prosperous, and the state's power declined day by day. In 375 BC, Marquis Ai of Han destroyed Zheng and moved his capital from Yangzhai to this place. In 230 BC, the state of Qin wiped out the state of Han, which had already existed for 145 years in the area of Zheng's capital.

On the site of the old capital of Zheng, the state of Han made some suitable adjustment for the capital. The royal palace and temple were rebuilt. The shape of the palace was a rectangle with an area of 1,720 thousand square meters. There were even some five-star shaped drain pipes, which were advanced at that time. There was also an east-west road about 5 meters wide. The road surface was flat and very hard. The more amazing thing was that the archaeologists also found the frozen room used in the palace, which had a height of about 3 meters. Five well-shaped basements formed in the room, and the surrounding area was covered with grass mixed with mud, and the bottom was filled with stones. In the western territory of the state of Han, an ancestral temple was discovered. This was a small city. There was a monumental stone tablet with the height of 3.26 meters, with the width of 0.45 meters in the middle.

几百年后，郑国风光不再，国势一天天衰落下去。公元前 375 年，韩哀侯消灭郑国，把自己的都城从阳翟迁到这里。一直到公元前 230 年，秦国灭亡韩国，韩国在郑国的都城立国达 145 年之久。

韩国在郑国旧都的基础上，对都城做了一些适合自己的修整。韩国重新修建了宫城和宗庙，宫城呈南北向长方形，面积为 172 万平方米，宫城里的排水设施甚至有五角形的排水管道，非常先进。宫城里还有一条宽约 5 米的东西大道，路面平整，非常坚硬。更为神奇的是，考古工作者还在宫城中发现了当时所用的冷藏室，高 3 米左右，室内形成 5 个井形地窖，其四周用草拌泥涂抹，底部用料礓石夯实。在韩国都城西部发现了韩国的宗庙，这是一座小城，里面有一座圭形碑，高 3.26 米，中部宽 0.45 米，中部偏下处有一个圆孔，这是在祭祀时用来系牺牲的。

韩国的申不害和韩非是中国古代著名的政治家和思想家。申不害主张刑名之学，加强君主专制，推行法制，重视农业，主张开荒，同时他还强调君主应该正直无私。韩哀侯曾拜申不害为相，结果韩国生产发展，军队强大，成为“战国七雄”之一。韩非思想先进，可惜韩国国君没有采纳。秦国国君极为欣赏他的思想和学说，邀请其入秦辅政，他的学说使得秦国很快统一全国。韩非的思想学说集先秦法家之大成，《韩非子》一书为先秦名著之一。

## 第五节　古都郑州历史名人轶事

郑州历史悠久，名人辈出，在中国历史上谱写了许多不朽的诗篇，为中华民族的创建、发展做出了杰出的贡献。

### 1. 轩辕黄帝一统华夏

黄帝是华夏部落联盟首领，中国远古时代华夏民族的共主。黄帝被尊

Under the middle part there was a round hole, which was used to tie the animals when doing sacrifice.

Shen Buhai and Han Fei were famous politicians and thinkers of Han in ancient times. Shen advocated the philosophy of the legal school, strengthened the autocratic monarchy, promoted the legal system, attached importance to agriculture, and advocated cultivating virgin land. At the same time, he also emphasized that the monarch should be upright and selfless. Marquis Ai of Han appointed Shen Buhai as his prime minister. As a result the state of Han developed very quickly, and the army became stronger. Finally it joined the Seven Strong States in the Warring States Period. Han Fei's thought was advanced, but the Monarch of Han didn't accept his ideas. Monarch of Qin greatly appreciated Han Fei's thoughts and doctrines and invited him to the State Qin to help. His theory unified Qin. Han Fei's ideological theory combined the thoughts of pre-Qin legalists. The book *Han Feizi* was one of the pre-Qin classics books.

## V. The Famous Historical Figures of Ancient Zhengzhou

With a long history and a large number of celebrities, Zhengzhou made outstanding contributions to the development of the Chinese nation.

**1.Yellow Emperor unifying Huaxia**

The Yellow Emperor was the leader of the ancient Chinese tribal alliance, the co-owner of the Chinese nation in ancient China. He was respected as the ancestor of the Chinese nation. His surname was Gongsun, and later changed to Ji. Because he lived on the hill of Xuanyuan and invented Xuanmian (the specially designed wagons and clothes for ancient officials), Yellow Emperor is also called Xuanyuan. He built capital Youxiong (now Xinzheng, Zhengzhou), so he was also known as Youxiong Shi.

In the later period of the Yan Emperor (Shennong), the various tribes of the Central Plains attacked each other and the wars lasted for a long time. The Yellow Emperor took the time to defeat the different tribes. The leaders of the remaining tribes submitted themselves to the trio of the Yan Emperor, the Yellow Emperor and Chiyou. The Yellow Emperor lived in the Central Plains. The Yan Emperor was in the West, the west of Mount Taihang; Chi You was the monarch of Jiuli, who

为中华民族“人文初祖”，本姓公孙，后改姬姓，居于轩辕之丘，又因他发明了轩冕，故被称为轩辕，号轩辕氏，建都于有熊，亦称有熊氏。

炎帝神农氏后期，中原各部族互相攻伐，战乱不止。黄帝乘时而起，打败不同的部族，其余部族的首领亦纷纷归附，于是形成炎帝、黄帝、蚩尤鼎足而立的局面，黄帝居中原，炎帝居太行山以西，蚩尤是九黎君主，居东方。黄帝以统一华夏部落与征服东夷、九黎族的伟绩载入史册。相传尧、舜、禹、皋陶、伯益、汤等均是他的后裔，因此黄帝被奉为中华民族的共同始祖。黄帝和炎帝时期逐渐形成华夏族，他们都被视为华夏民族共同的祖先，故中国人自称“炎黄子孙”。

人们每年在陕西黄帝陵举行祭祀活动，在河南新郑市举行拜祖活动。2008 年，国务院确定新郑黄帝拜祖祭典为第一批国家级非物质文化遗产扩展项目。黄帝故里拜祖大典，弘扬了中华民族优秀传统文化，缅怀始祖功德，突出了中华民族寻根拜祖的主题，象征着炎黄子孙血脉相连、薪火相传。

## 2. 大禹治水过家门而不入

大禹治水是中国古代的神话传说故事。大禹是黄帝的后代，三皇五帝时期，黄河泛滥，鲧、禹父子二人受命于尧、舜二帝，任崇伯和夏伯，负责治水。鲧治水无方，水患更加严重。后来由禹率领民众治水，最终获得了胜利。面对滔滔洪水，大禹从鲧治水的失败中汲取教训，改变了“堵”的办法，对洪水进行疏导，体现出他具有带领人民战胜困难的聪明才智。大禹为了治理洪水，长年在外与民众一起奋战，置个人利益于不顾，“三过家门而不入”。大禹治水 13 年，耗尽心血与体力，终于完成了治水的大业。大禹“三过家门而不入”的故事，体现了他公而忘私的高尚情操。

was living in the East. The Yellow Emperor is historically known for unifying the Huaxia tribe and conquering Dongyi and Jiuli. According to legend, Yao, Shun, Yu, Gaoyao, Boyi, Tang, etc. are all his descendants, so the Yellow Emperor was regarded as the common ancestor of the Chinese nation. During the Yellow Emperor and Yan Emperor period, the Huaxia people gradually formed. They were regarded as the common ancestor of the Huaxia people. Therefore, the Chinese claimed to be "the Descendants of the Emperor Yan and Huang".

Every year, a ritual activity is held in the Mausoleum of the Yellow Emperor in Shaanxi Province, and there is a worship activity in Xinzheng City, Henan Province. In 2008, the State Council determined that the worship ceremony of the Yellow Emperor in Xinzheng was the first batch of expansion projects of national intangible cultural heritage. In the hometown of the Yellow Emperor, many activities are carried out such as the ancestral worship and the promotion of the outstanding traditional culture of the Chinese nation. The people's beliefs are deeply rooted in its ancestors symbolizing the blood relationship of the descendants of Yan Emperor and Yellow Emperor.

**2. Yu: Ancient God of Flood Control**

Yu's story of controlling flood is a mythical legend of ancient China. He was the descendant of the Yellow Emperor. During the Three Emperors and Five Sovereigns, the Yellow River flooded. Gun and his son Yu were appointed by the Emperor Yao and the Emperor Shun as Chongbo and Xiabo to control floods. As Gun failed to control the floods, Yu led people to combat the flood waters. Facing the floods, Yu learned lessons from the failure of Gun's way of water control, changed the way of "blocking", and used dredging measures. These methods reflected his ingenuity in leading the people to overcome difficulties. He was so dedicated that it was said that he passed his home three times and did not enter the door when he passed by. After thirteen years of continuous efforts, Yu succeeded in dredging all the rivers and doing away with the evil of flood. Yu's story is a manifestation of the noble sentiment of selflessness.

**3. Duke Zhuang of Zheng as a Great Ruler during Spring and Autumn Period**

Duke Zhuang of Zheng (757 BC-701 BC), whose family name was Ji, and given name was Wusheng, was the son of Duke Wu, a famous politician in the early Spring and Autumn Period. He was called "the leader of the three rulers during the Spring and Autumn Period", and he was the third monarch of Zheng. After King

### 3. 春秋首霸郑庄公

郑庄公 ( 前 757—前 701)，姬姓，郑氏，名寤生，郑武公之子，春秋初期著名的政治家，被称为“春秋三小霸之首”，是郑国第 3 位国君。自周平王东迁后，周室衰弱，诸侯国逐渐强大。郑庄公把自己事业的立足点坚决地放置于郑国，不惜与自己的弟弟、母亲以武力相对抗，与周天子闹翻也决不动摇，他以极大的精力经营自己的国家，终使郑国成为东周初期崭露头角的诸侯国。繻葛之战后，周天子威信扫地，郑庄公声威大振，宋、卫、陈等宿敌都来求和，郑国成为当时中原最强盛的诸侯国。公元前 701 年，郑庄公与齐、卫、宋等大国诸侯结盟，俨然已是诸侯霸主。郑庄公凭借自己的智谋和权术扮演了一个特殊的角色，对当时社会政治趋势的演化具有促进作用。

### 4. 郑国子产不毁乡校

子产（？—前 522），春秋时期著名政治家、思想家，历史典籍以其字“子产”为通称，又称公孙侨、公孙成子、国侨等。政治思想上，子产“择能而使”的用人观、“不毁乡校”体现的民本思想、“宽猛相济”的治国理念等均传于后世；法律思想上，由于铸刑书于鼎以及对子太叔的遗嘱，子产和管仲一起被视作法家先驱，甚至被某些学者认为是“法家思想之始”；在生态观方面，子产注意保护林木，《吕氏春秋》记载子产相郑期间，种植并严格管理行道树，“桃李之垂于行者，莫之援也”。因此，子产堪称春秋时执政者的楷模。

### 5. 韩非集法家之大成

韩非是战国时期韩国都城新郑（今河南省新郑市）人，法家代表人

Ping of Zhou had moved eastward, the State of Zhou became weaker and weaker, but other vassal states gradually grew stronger. Duke Zhuang of Zheng firmly placed his foothold in Zheng, and he did not hesitate to resist against his brother and mother by force. He didn't yield to King Zhou. He ruled his country with great energy and finally made the State of Zheng a promising vassal state in the early days of the Eastern Zhou Dynasty. After the battle of Xuge, King Zhou lost his prestige, and Duke Zhuang of Zheng gained great fame. The states of Song, Wei, Chen and other enemies came to seek peace, and Zheng became the most powerful vassal state in the Central Plains at that time. In 701 BC, Duke Zhuang of Zheng allied with other vassal states like Qi, Wei, Song and Duke Zhuang of Zheng became the lord at that time. Duke Zhuang of Zheng played a special role with his own wisdom and power, and promoted the evolution of social and political trends at that time.

**4. Zichan of Zheng as a pioneering reformer**

Zichan (?-522 BC) was a famous politician and thinker during the Spring and Autumn Period. Zichan appeared in the historical books, generally known as "Gongsun Qiao", "Gongsun Chengzi", and "Guoqiao". In political thoughts, some of his concepts are passed on to the generation, such as the concept of employing people with "selection of ability" , the people-oriented concept of "not destroying the township school" and the concept of using a proper mixture of severity and gentleness in ruling a country. According to the casting words on the tripod and Zitaishu's will, Zichan and Guan Zhong are considered as the pioneers of the legal thoughts. Some scholars even regard them as the "original founders of the legal thought". In terms of ecological outlook, Zichan pays attention to the protection of forest. In the *Lüshi Chunqiu* (*Master Lü's Spring and Autumn Annals*), Zichan was recorded of planting and managing the street trees, such as the saying goes, "The peaches and plums are hanging on the walkers, which is a help for them". Zichan was a good example of the rulers during Spring and Autumn Period.

**5. Han Fei is the most famous figure in Legal Thought**

Han Fei was from the State of Han's capital Xinzheng (now Xinzheng City, Henan Province), a representative of legal thought, an outstanding thinker, philosopher and essayist.

Han Fei combined Shang Yang's law concept, Shen Buhai's methods, and Shen Dao's concept of power. He was the master of the legal thought. He also integrated

物，杰出的思想家、哲学家和散文家。

韩非将商鞅的“法”、申不害的“术”和慎到的“势”集于一身，是法家思想的集大成者。韩非还将老子的辩证法、朴素唯物主义与法融为一体。韩非创立的法家学说，为中国第一个统一专制的中央集权制国家的诞生提供了理论依据。他的文章在先秦诸子散文中独树一帜，极为重视唯物主义与效益主义思想，积极倡导君主专制主义理论，目的是为专制君主提供富国强兵的理论依据。

《史记》载，秦王见《孤愤》《五蠹》之书，曰：“嗟乎，寡人得见此人与之游，死不得恨矣！”可见当时秦王对韩非的重视。韩非的思想对中国影响深远，历来的儒法之争都可见其思想的威力。

### 6.“诗圣”杜甫留史诗

杜甫，字子美，汉族，原籍湖北襄阳，后来迁到河南巩义。他自号少陵野老，是唐代伟大的现实主义诗人，与李白合称“李杜”。为了与另两位诗人李商隐与杜牧即“小李杜”区别，杜甫与李白又合称“大李杜”，杜甫也常被称为“老杜”。后世称其杜拾遗、杜工部，也称他为杜少陵、杜草堂。

杜甫创作了《登高》《春望》《北征》《三吏》《三别》等名作，他的诗歌具有强烈的现实性，他所生活的时代所发生的事情几乎都被他以诗歌的形式记录了下来。杜甫的思想核心是儒家的仁政思想，他有“致君尧舜上，再使风俗淳”的宏伟抱负。杜甫虽然在世时名声并不显赫，但后来声名远播，对中国文学和日本文学都产生了深远的影响。杜甫对中国古典诗歌的影响非常深远，被后人称为“诗圣”，他的诗被称为“诗史”。杜甫共有约1500首诗歌被保留了下来，大多集于《杜工部集》。

the dialectics of Lao-tzu, naive materialism and law together. The law theory was founded by Han Fei which provided a theoretical basis for the birth of China's first unified centralized bureaucratic state. His articles had unique features in the prose before the Qin Dynasty, which attached great importance to materialism and utilitarianism, and actively advocated for an authoritative monarchy. The purpose was to provide the authoritarian monarch with the idea of enriching the country and strengthening the soldiers.

It is stated in *Shi Ji* (*Records of the Historian*) that when the King of Qin read the book *Lonely Indignation* and *Five Poems*, he said, "Oh, if I meet this person and take a tour with him, there will be no regret in my life." Han Fei was so important in the King of Qin's eyes at that time. His thoughts have influenced China profoundly. Historically, the disputes between Confucianism and Law have shown the power of his thoughts.

**6. "Poetry Saint" Du Fu**

Du Fu, also known as Zimei, was born in Xiangyang, Hubei. He later moved to Gongyi, Henan. He gave himself a name of Shaoling Yelao. He was a great realist poet of the Tang Dynasty. Li Bai and he were called "Li and Du". In order to distinguish it from the other two poets, Li Shangyin and Du Mu, who were called "Junior Li and Du", Du Fu and Li Bai are also collectively referred to "Senior Li and Du", and Du Fu is often referred to as "Old Du". Later generations called him Du Shiyi, Du Gongbu, Du Shaoling and Du Caotang according to his official position and private cabinet.

Du Fu created famous poems such as *On the Height*, *Spring View*, *Journey to the North*, *Three Officials* and *Three Departures*. His poems reflected the reality of the society, and almost everything that happened in his life had been recorded in the form of poetry. The core of Du Fu's thought is the Confucian benevolent ideology. He has the grand ambition of assisting the ruler to adopt the ways of Emperor Yao and Shun and build an honest and peaceful society. Although Du Fu was not famous when he was alive, he later became well known and had a profound influence on Chinese and Japanese literature. Du Fu's influence in Chinese classical poetry is very far-reaching. He is reserved as a "Poetry Saint" by people, and his poems are called "Poetry History". Du Fu left some 1,500 poems, which have been collected in *The Anthology of Du Gongbu*.

**附录**
Appendix

## 中国历史年代简表
## A Brief Chronology of Chinese History

<table>
<tr><td colspan="2" rowspan="5">五帝时代<br>Period of the Five Legendary Rulers<br>c. 2600 BC-c. 2070 BC</td><td>黄帝 Huangdi (Yellow Emperor)</td></tr>
<tr><td>颛顼 Zhuanxu</td></tr>
<tr><td>帝喾 Diku (Emperor Ku)</td></tr>
<tr><td>尧 Yao</td></tr>
<tr><td>舜 Shun</td></tr>
<tr><td colspan="2">夏 Xia Dynasty</td><td>c. 2070 BC-c. 1600 BC</td></tr>
<tr><td colspan="2">商 Shang Dynasty</td><td>c. 1600 BC-c. 1046 BC</td></tr>
<tr><td colspan="2">西周 Western Zhou Dynasty</td><td>c. 1046 BC-c. 771 BC</td></tr>
<tr><td rowspan="2">东周<br>Eastern Zhou Dynasty<br>770 BC-256 BC</td><td>春秋<br>Spring and Autumn Period</td><td>770 BC-476 BC</td></tr>
<tr><td>战国<br>Warring States Period</td><td>475 BC-221 BC</td></tr>
<tr><td colspan="2">秦 Qin Dynasty</td><td>221 BC-206 BC</td></tr>
<tr><td rowspan="2">汉<br>Han Dynasty<br>206 BC-220 AD</td><td>西汉 Western Han</td><td>206 BC-25 AD</td></tr>
<tr><td>东汉 Eastern Han</td><td>25 AD-220 AD</td></tr>
<tr><td rowspan="3">三国<br>Three Kingdoms<br>220 AD-280 AD</td><td>魏 Wei</td><td>220 AD-265 AD</td></tr>
<tr><td>蜀汉 Shu Han</td><td>221 AD-263 AD</td></tr>
<tr><td>吴 Wu</td><td>222 AD-280 AD</td></tr>
<tr><td rowspan="2">晋<br>Jin Dynasty<br>265 AD–420 AD</td><td>西晋 Western Jin</td><td>265 AD-317 AD</td></tr>
<tr><td>东晋 Eastern Jin</td><td>317 AD-420 AD</td></tr>
</table>

**续表 Continued Table**

| | | | |
|---|---|---|---|
| 南北朝<br>Southern and<br>Northern Dynasties<br>420 AD-589 AD | 南朝<br>Southern Dynasties | 宋 Song | 420 AD-479 AD |
| | | 齐 Qi | 479 AD-502 AD |
| | | 梁 Liang | 502 AD-557 AD |
| | | 陈 Chen | 557 AD-589 AD |
| | 北朝<br>Northern Dynasties | 北魏<br>Northern Wei | 386 AD-534 AD |
| | | 东魏<br>Eastern Wei | 534 AD-550 AD |
| | | 北齐<br>Northern Qi | 550 AD-577 AD |
| | | 西魏<br>Western Wei | 535 AD-556 AD |
| | | 北周<br>Northern Zhou | 557 AD-581 AD |
| 隋 Sui Dynasty | | 581 AD-618 AD | |
| 唐 Tang Dynasty | | 618 AD-907 AD | |
| 五代十国<br>Five Dynasties and<br>Ten States | 五代<br>Five Dynasties<br>907 AD-960 AD | 后梁 Later Liang | 907 AD-923 AD |
| | | 后唐 Later Tang | 923 AD-936 AD |
| | | 后晋 Later Jin | 936 AD-947 AD |
| | | 后汉 Later Han | 947 AD-950 AD |
| | | 后周 Later Zhou | 951 AD-960 AD |
| | 十国<br>Ten States<br>902 AD-979 AD | 北汉 Northern Han | 951 AD-979 AD |
| | | 吴 Wu | 902 AD-937 AD |
| | | 吴越 Wuyue | 907 AD-978 AD |
| | | 闽 Min | 909 AD-945 AD |
| | | 南汉 Southern Han | 917 AD-971 AD |
| | | 荆南(又称“南平”)<br>Jingnan (Nanping) | 924 AD-963 AD |
| | | 楚 Chu | 927 AD-951 AD |
| | | 南唐 Southern Tang | 937 AD-975 AD |
| | | 前蜀 Former Shu | 907 AD-925 AD |
| | | 后蜀 Later Shu | 934 AD-965 AD |

续表 Continued Table

| | | |
|---|---|---|
| 宋<br>Song Dynasty<br>960 AD-1279 AD | 北宋<br>Northern Song | 960 AD-1127 AD |
| | 南宋<br>Southern Song | 1127 AD-1279 AD |
| 辽<br>Liao (契丹 Qidan/Khitan) | 907 AD-1125 AD | |
| 金 Jin | 1115 AD-1234 AD | |
| 西夏 Xixia (Tangut) | 1038 AD-1227 AD | |
| 元 Yuan Dynasty | 1206 AD-1368 AD | |
| 明 Ming Dynasty | 1368 AD-1644 AD | |
| 清 Qing Dynasty | 1616 AD-1911 AD | |
| 中华民国<br>Republic of China | 1912 AD-1949 AD | |
| 中华人民共和国<br>People's Republic of China | 1949 AD- | |